Even Though

H.J. WEILER

The Holy Bible, New International Version Copyright C 1978 by New York Bible Society

The New Testament, New International Version

C 1973 by New York Bible Society International

C 1978 by New York International Bible Society

Portions of this Bible have been previously published under the following copyrights by the New York international Bible Society. The Book of John c 1970; The Book of Isaiah c 1975; The Book of Daniel c 1976; Proverbs and Ecclesiastes c 1977

Library of Congress Catalog Card Number 78-69799

Published by Zondervan Corporation

Grand Rapids, Michigan 49506, USA

ISBN: 979-8-89694-263-4 - Paperback
ISBN: 979-8-89694-262-7 - eBook

DEDICATION

This book is dedicated to every person who provided me with help, resources, and opportunities, and to my husband Robert. I cherish our time together. Thank you for believing in me.

Whatever you can do, or dream you can, begin it.
Boldness has genius, power and magic in it.

— Johann Wolfgang von Goethe

These are the events as I remember them. The names and places have been changed.

CONTENTS

Introduction 1

Determined to Progress 3

Things are not always as they appear 10

Staying the Course...16

Beginning Again..22

Pressing On 28

Growing Up – For Real this Time.................................. 34

The Sweet Spot 44

The Unthinkable 51

Good, Bad, and Ugly...62

A New Beginning 73

There are no obstacles, only opportunities......................79

The Relentless Pursuit of Constant and Gradual Improvement 97

Decisions and the end of an Era.....................................104

Progress In Spite of Setbacks... 111

Gratitude 119

A New Mindset 123

A New Hope..130

Beyond my Wildest Dreams 139

Joy in Spite of Adversity...147

Freedom... 153

Acknowledgement..163

About the author..167

INTRODUCTION

"For I know the plans I have for you, declares the Lord, plans to prosper you and not to harm you, plans to give you hope and a future" (Jer 29:11 NIV).

My father bought me a bicycle the year I turned five, as I had outgrown the little red pedal car I had been riding around the neighbourhood. The pedal car had a trailer so I could take my treasures with me. I loved it! It was a sad day when my car was gone, and no longer waiting to share great adventures with me. The bicycle was intriguing. It was a used bicycle, and my father diligently fixed it up, even painting it red, like my pedal car. Even with the training wheels, the bicycle outpaced the pedal car and I quickly forgot about my beloved pedal car, and embraced my bicycle.

There were other kids in the neighbourhood riding bicycles without training wheels, and the day came for mine to come off. My father held on to the seat of the bicycle while I pedalled at an impressive clip (compared to the pedal car anyway). Thinking my dad must be a great runner to be able to keep up with me, I turned around to see how he was managing, and much to my surprise he was *way* back there. I was riding all by myself! And then I promptly crashed. Back

1

up on the bicycle I went, until I could ride without crashing. I felt free as a bird.

My bicycle was a big part of my life. I outgrew it and received a brand new red one with three speeds when I was about ten years old. I loved it. I wanted to do something great with my life, and when I rode my bicycle, I felt like that might be possible, like I could do anything.

When I started junior high, I rode my bicycle to school— it took almost a half hour to walk there, but I could make it in ten minutes on my bicycle. There were some really nice bicycles on the school bike rack, and I decided I'd like to level up my bicycle. I found a used ten speed racing bicycle for sale. It was from Sears, so nothing special. But it had racing handlebars, and ten speeds. I had been saving my allowance money and wanted to spend it on this bicycle. My father took me to buy it, and again, he diligently worked to fix it. This one he painted metallic blue, to my delight. I rode that bicycle everywhere—downtown, to the mall, to school, to my friend's houses. Everywhere! I was so grateful to my father for buying me a bicycle, fixing it for me and teaching me how to ride. I was a very introverted, solitary girl, so riding a bicycle was a perfect activity for me. I felt like my mother wished I hadn't been born, so I took every opportunity to leave the house and ride my bicycle.

This book tells my story—a nobody from nowhere. It is full of ups and downs, joy and sorrow. Just a very human experience. My hope is that you will see aspects of your own life in the pages that follow, that as you read, you will be encouraged to keep pressing on, keep growing, keep learning, and keep becoming a better version of yourself. You deserve the best!

Enjoy the ride.

DETERMINED TO PROGRESS

"The Lord your God is with you, He is mighty to save. He will take great delight in you, He will quiet you with His love, He will rejoice over you with singing" (Zeph 3:17 NIV).

"You have to be kidding me," I thought. It was the early 1980's and I was 14 years old. My mother took me to Woolco—a discount retail store— to get some new clothes. I had tried on several different things, but this time when I came out of the changing room, my mother was gone. I figured she was in the clothing department somewhere, so I wandered around looking for her. When I didn't find her, I put my own clothes back on and looked further into the store. Still nothing. With a growing sense of panic, I went out to the parking lot. To my shock and disbelief, the car was gone. My mother had left me at the mall.

As that reality set in, I recalled a time when I was about five. I was tired of repeatedly feeling unloved and unwanted, so I decided to run away from home. Mother was lying on the couch reading, and I went to the front door with my packed bag and announced I was leaving home.

Mother curtly replied, "I don't have time for this nonsense. Put your stuff away." I don't think I was *really* going to leave home, I just wanted to convey that I felt there wasn't much point in my being there, since mother couldn't be bothered with me.

Mother apparently still couldn't be bothered with me, because she had just left me at the mall. There were no cell phones then, so I decided to walk home. It was about a 45 minute walk. When I got home, she was there making supper. I went straight to my room in silence. I had already learned that if I spoke, I would be yelled at and blamed, and end up feeling worse than I already did. "Suck it up, buttercup," I said to myself.

I learned to just say nothing after the time I had asked if Sheila, my friend from church, could sleep overnight and mother refused. I explained that I had been overnight at Sheila's several times, and was feeling bad because Sheila had never been to our house. Mother then grabbed me by the shoulders and started banging me against the wall, yelling what a selfish, rotten kid I was. My dad sat on the couch doing his crossword puzzle and said nothing, so I thought that her behaviour was acceptable, or that I wasn't worth defending. I had only asked if I could have a friend overnight and explained how I felt about the situation.

After the banging stopped, I noticed the drywall had cracked. With nothing else to do but leave, I went to my room. I decided that I wouldn't bother speaking next time. History had taught me there would be a next time. I felt worthless, frightened, and sad, which felt worse than not being allowed to have Sheila sleep over. Asking for things generally didn't go well, so the things I asked for were few and far between.

I wish I knew then that my mother's behaviour was her problem, *not my fault*. I did learn eventually. When I was in my early 50's, while speaking with my dad, I told him about the time mother left me at the mall. He didn't know about that, but he did tell me that she had left him at church soon after they had been married. It was winter time, and he wasn't properly dressed to walk home in the snow and cold. Some people he knew happened to be driving by, saw him walking, and offered him a ride home. He didn't know what would have become of him if he hadn't received that ride. Having that conversation with my dad, many years after the day mother left me at the mall, helped me see my experience differently. I felt sad that my dad went through that, but my inner 14 year old self was comforted. That was just how mother was. It was nothing personal.

One summer, my favourite aunt—my dad's younger sister—and my uncle were visiting from Calgary, which was two time zones away. They visited my home every so often to see their parents and siblings. Auntie and Unc invited me to Calgary to stay with them for a couple of weeks the following July, and go to the Calgary Stampede. Calgary is sometimes referred to as Texas North. The stampede would have a rodeo, barrel racing, and chuck wagon racing, to name only a few of the events. I would have loved to stay with Auntie and Unc, and also go to the stampede to see all kinds of things I had never seen before. And the horses! I loved horses. What a lovely invitation. I was thrilled not only about the prospect of going to the stampede, watching the events and seeing all the horses, but the fact that they actually *wanted* me to come and be with me for a couple of weeks was almost dizzying. A far cry from the inconvenience I felt like at home.

The only problem was, I was afraid to go. I was just a kid and I was afraid to fly on an airplane by myself. I had never been on an airplane before. The fast pace of the big city was scary enough, and that was where the only airport was. Besides that, airfare would cost money, and my parents didn't have much of that. I was certain they wouldn't want to spend money on a plane ticket for me to have the time of my life with my aunt and uncle in Calgary. So I declined their most kind and wonderful offer. I would spend the rest of my life being sorry about that decision. If I had it to do over again, I would choose Calgary.

Life continued. I went to school, cleaned the kitchen after supper, and sometimes babysat my sister, who was six years younger than me. Since I ended up not getting clothes at Woolco that day, I decided to get a *job* so I could buy my own clothes. I could take the bus to and from the mall, shop with my friends, and not feel like a *less than, not enough, waste of time, no-one will ever want you* loser by potentially being left at the mall by my mother again.

I scoured the classified section of the newspaper for jobs. As luck would have it, McDonald's was building a new restaurant right down the road from our church. The new McDonald's was set to open in a few months. I had just turned 15. I talked to my parents about it and my mother flatly refused to drive me to or from work, even though I offered to pay her for gas. She worked part time at the library, so I couldn't understand why she couldn't drive me. It seemed to me it wasn't a case of *couldn't*, it was more of a case of *wouldn't*. I realized the new McDonald's was on the other side of town, on the highway headed out of town, but I figured if we could drive out there to church, why couldn't we drive out there to take me to work?

Feeling devastated and trapped, I went back to my room. I was beginning to feel that my mother did not want me to succeed. Whose mother doesn't want them to be successful? I felt a growing sense of shame and spent more time in my room. What was wrong with me that my mother had gone beyond treating me like an inconvenience to actively sabotaging my growth and success? As I was trying to figure out what to do next, maybe get a job closer to home so I could take the city bus or something, my dad came to my room.

My high school was downtown, just like the Grey Coach bus terminal. He suggested if I had after school shifts at McDonald's I could walk to the Grey Coach station and buy a ticket. Then when the bus approached the new McDonald's on the highway, I could politely ask the driver to stop and let me out, even though there wasn't a stop there. Dad said he would pick me up when the shift ended at 8:00 pm, as he would be home from work by then. He also said he would drive me to and from work on the weekends. I was very grateful to him for that, so I applied for the job and was hired. Finally, some progress. I had my own job and could earn my own money, buy my own things, and didn't need to ask my mother for them.

I did a couple of training sessions at a different McDonald's location from the one I was hired for, as it wasn't finished being built quite yet. The training location was a loud, busy place with lots of teenage workers rushing around in a small workspace. Since I would be working at a different location, I wouldn't be working with any of those people, and the location of things probably wouldn't be exactly the same. All the workers seemed confident in what they were doing, so I pressed through my fear and tried to pay attention and learn what I was being taught about my job, expecting that some day soon I too would be confidently rushing around in a small space doing my job with excellence and making friends with the other workers.

The new McDonald's on the highway was soon open and I was scheduled to work! I packed my uniform in my school bag and took it with me to school. After school, I walked to the Grey Coach terminal with a growing sense of dread. It was dirty, creepy, and scary. I was afraid to ask the driver to stop and let me out when there was no stop. I was afraid I would be late for my new job. I was angry that I had to spend a full hour of my pay on a bus ticket just to get to work. But I was determined to make my own way and not be held back or controlled by my mother. I would *not* spend the rest of my life in my room!

I did go shopping with my friend, bought new clothes, and got my ears pierced, which I wasn't allowed to do. My friend and I went to the Merle Norman kiosk in the mall and learned how to apply makeup. I bought some makeup. I was starting to feel like I would make it. Unfortunately, there was lots of yelling when the earrings were discovered. I guess the kind woman at the Merle Norman kiosk did a good job of teaching my friend and me about makeup, as nothing was said about it.

My dad had a conversation with his elder sister about my earrings. She thought it was fine for me to have my ears pierced and wondered what all the fuss was about. Shortly thereafter, my mother and then eight year old sister had their ears pierced too. Funny how my earrings caused yelling, and dad all but drove my mother and sister to the mall to have theirs done. I was angry about what felt like two sets of rules. Perhaps it wasn't two sets of rules. Perhaps it was leadership. I knew what I wanted, took action to get it, and paved the way for others to do the same. I loved that I had been successful in my attempt to become me, and had begun to develop my own voice.

Even though I was afraid of taking the bus from the creepy Grey Coach station, angry I had to spend a full of hour my own pay for a bus ticket to get to work because my mother wouldn't drive me, afraid I would make mistakes in my job and get in trouble, and worried that I would not know my work colleagues, I was glad to know that God was with me, that He delighted in me, and He rejoiced over me. I felt in need of saving, and God was mighty to save. I would be alright.

THINGS ARE NOT ALWAYS AS THEY APPEAR

"…no eye has seen, no ear has heard, no mind can conceive what God has planned for those who love him" (1 Cor 2:9 NIV).

The McDonald's where I worked opened in the spring of 1984. Everyone was either newly hired or transferred from another location, so unless people knew each other from school, nobody knew anybody. As I was only 15, I was hired to work the French fry station and clean the lobby. I could work the cash register when I turned 16. I'm not sure if that was a McDonald's rule or a self-imposed rule. Either way, I was a "fry girl." As a result, I was only scheduled during lunch on the weekend, so I only worked every Saturday for the first several months.

One Saturday that summer, while I was working, there was this guy cleaning behind one of the grills in the back, and of course the grill was pulled out. The grill was in my way. I tried to edge past it, but he graciously pushed the grill back in so I could get by. I could tell by the way he looked at me that he liked me. I could also tell he was older than me—he had a moustache. A proper moustache, not the peach-fuzz that most 15 year old guys had. I was beside myself with glee. An older-than-me guy, who was cute, was interested in *me*? I was used to being invisible, and figured no one would ever be interested in me.

I decided to test out my theory. Was the grill guy actually interested in me, or was he just being polite? I found fake reasons to go by where he was working, and he continued to patiently pull the grill in and out so I could get by. He looked intrigued, not annoyed, which intrigued me.

A few weeks later, the grill guy and I worked the same shift again. He told me his name was Rob and asked me my name and my phone number. I gave him both. I wondered if he would still be interested in me when he found out I was only 15. Our McDonald's was on the highway between two cities, and he lived in the other city, so we did not go to the same school. He didn't ask me how old I was, to my relief.

Days passed and I wondered if he would call. He did! We had long chats on the phone a few times every week. I found him to be interesting, different, and refreshing. He liked race cars and airplanes. He was fun and funny. Every time the phone rang my heart jumped because I wondered if it would be him. I cherished the time I spent talking with him.

Later that fall, Rob asked me to be his girlfriend. I had been hoping that he would ask, and when he finally did, I said yes! I was crazy about him and still shocked that he was interested in me. I remember going to an extended family Thanksgiving that year, feeling like things would be OK for me. I had a job, some new clothes, and a boyfriend. My mother's grip on me was loosening, and I loved it.

Rob was two years older than me, but he was ok with our age gap. We didn't see each other often, as we lived in different cities, but we talked on the phone a lot. My parents got "call waiting" on their phone service because I was on the phone so much. I would write notes to Rob and leave them in his locker at work. He recorded audio cassette tapes and left them in my locker. I loved playing those tapes, hearing his voice, and having him tell me he loved me. He called me his "crazy diamond." His parents did their grocery shopping on Saturdays at the mall where my mother left me. Sometimes he would go with his parents to the grocery store/mall, and I would take the bus there. We would hang around at the mall together and go back to his house. I stayed for supper and we played board games in the evening. My dad would come and pick me up.

Rob loved bicycling too, and the following summer, we rode our bicycles to each other's house and spent time together when we weren't working. It took about half an hour for us to ride our bicycles to each other's house. Once, we decided to ride our bicycles to the small town of Two Rivers, about a 30 minute drive south of where Rob lived. That was going to be a very long bicycle ride, but I was eager to spend the whole day with Rob. However, about halfway to our destination, I developed a mechanical problem with my bicycle, and I was stuck in second gear. We decided to head back home rather than continue on. It was a very slow ride home being stuck in such a low gear. At least the bicycle worked at all—having a total mechanical failure would have really been a problem.

Rob was also part of a youth group at a church in his village. His youth pastor lived in my city, and would pick me up and take me to the youth meetings. It was wonderful to spend time with Rob, and I was madly in love with him. He even gave me a beautiful ruby and diamond promise ring. We planned to get married when we were old enough.

Our love was wonderful. A popular song on the radio at that time was "You're the Inspiration," by a band called Chicago. I loved the song and suggested that it could be "our song." Rob agreed, and so it was.

Things continued in this wonderful way. Rob saved his money and bought a car so we could see each other more often. Sometimes he brought me roses. Sometimes he would be waiting for me when I finished school, and we would drive around. Rob loved cars, Formula 1 Racing, and driving. I loved being with him. My heart would skip a beat when I saw him waiting for me after school.

One summer Rob and I went to a former Formula 1 racetrack a couple of hours drive from our city. All kinds of cars raced there, and the pits were just tents, so we could get an up-close view of the cars and the people working on them. It was exciting to see car racing in real life, and the sound was amazing. It was wonderful to be with Rob for such a long time, and to see him at an event that he loved. That day at the racetrack, I bought a Rothman's Porsche t-shirt. It was thick and soft with half sleeves, white with blue letters and gold trim. That t-shirt was special to me, and I didn't want it to wear out, so I hardly ever wore it.

As time passed, Rob was promoted to manager at McDonald's and transferred to another location. Management didn't like the idea of us working together when he was a manager, even though I worked extra hard when we worked together so no one could say anything about him favouring me. That was the beginning of the end. By then, we had been together for over two years. He was 19 and I was 17. He met new people at his new McDonald's location. I could tell things were changing. I wrote him a poem and sent it to him in the mail—yes, snail mail—since we didn't work together anymore and I couldn't leave it in his locker at work. I hoped he would remember our love. It was the only poem I ever wrote. It was called Memories.

Memories

They loved each other so much. He was so masculine,
and yet so sensitive. And she was beautiful—
like a china doll.

Together, they walked through the woods
on warm autumn days, the wind whispering
in the trees. Their laughter was loud as
they soaked each other on hot summer days
while they washed his car.
And they sat by the fire together
on cold winter nights—their eyes sparkling.

One day, he left her.
He left her to walk through the woods,
on warm autumn days, the crackling of the leaves
echoing hopelessly. And on hot summer days
to hear traces of laughter drifting through the
silent air. And to sit by the fire on cold
winter nights with nothing—
except memories.

I think the poem struck him somehow, because he came to my house one evening and was very attentive. The poem apparently didn't have any lasting value as far as reminding him about our love was concerned, because one evening he came to my house after his shift. He informed me that he didn't love me anymore, and that he wanted to date someone else. At least he had the guts to tell me instead of cheat on me. To say I felt devastated would be an understatement. My heart was broken into a million pieces. I couldn't eat, couldn't sleep. I just stayed in my room and cried. I guessed it was all too good to be true. Maybe I really was a *less than, not enough, waste of time, no one will ever want you* loser. What happened? What went wrong? I had no idea.

Nothing seemed to make sense. From where I sat with my broken heart, it seemed hard to believe that it was inconceivable what God had prepared for me, at least in a good way. It was inconceivable to me that my wonderful relationship with Rob was over. God was about love and hope and prosperity, about amazing things that had never been done before. What could those things possibly be?

STAYING THE COURSE

"Give thanks in all circumstances, for this is God's will for you in Christ Jesus" (1 Thess 5:18 NIV).

The news about my break up spread through our McDonalds like wildfire. I went to school everyday, and walked to the creepy Grey Coach bus terminal a couple of times a week to get to my shift at McDonalds. I managed to do all of that without bursting into tears, but I'm certain everyone could tell how miserable I was.

A girl at school, Sherri, who also worked at our Mc Donald's, had recently broken up with her longtime boyfriend, so she certainly recognized my body language. I didn't know her well, but we had the same lunch hour and I saw her in the cafeteria one day. She was an absolute angel. She invited me to her apartment where she lived with her mother. She had a driver's license and a car. I had neither. We went shopping and bought some new things, and I was profoundly grateful for her kindness during the most difficult time in my life (to that point). She knew how devastated I felt. She understood and told me I would be ok. I had my doubts.

In any case, I had my hair cut. It was a bit spiky and funky and different. I needed to reinvent myself, and I thought a new haircut would help with that. I began to notice that guys noticed me. That was something I had never noticed before, except for Rob. One time I was telling my father that I was "pretty good" at something. His response was, "Yes, you are pretty, but not as strikingly beautiful as your sister." *What?* That comment left me feeling like a *less than, not enough, waste of time, no one will ever want you* loser. I was 17, fit from cycling, and had a spiky, funky new hair cut. And guys were noticing me. Maybe my father was wrong.

A couple of months passed, and just as I began to figure I would survive, Rob called and said he was sorry and had made a mistake. He wanted to be with me again. I generally felt invisible, misunderstood, alone, and worthless. When I was with Rob, I felt alive, that I had value, and was worth spending time with.

Herein lies the problem many of us have; we rely on acceptance or approval from *external* sources instead of ourselves. Too bad I didn't know that then. If I had liked myself, and believed in myself, being confident that I had worth and value regardless of whether or not people approved of me, I might not have been so devastated. The sad part is that I didn't think I was good enough. I *was* good enough, I just didn't know it.

I hoped things would return to normal, so I agreed to get back together with him. Unfortunately, the damage was done and things were just not the same. I kept expecting the other shoe to drop, and drop, it did.

Over the next two years or so, we had an on again/off again relationship. It was always Rob who wanted out of the relationship, only to change his mind a short time later and want to come back. Every time we broke up and got back together, I hoped it would be different, and things would be like they were in the beginning. But they never were the same. Each time this happened, I felt more and more like the *less than, not enough, waste of time, no one will ever want you* loser I was trying desperately not to be.

In my last year of high school, I scored in the 98th percentile in an aptitude test for filing. I was *not* impressed. I had visions of myself being chained to a file cart for the rest of my life and wondered how I could possibly make a decent living that way.

I decided I wanted to go to a local university to study business administration. I could live at home, which would keep the expenses under control, since I would need to pay for school myself. Except that I needed an 80 percent average to get in, and six math credits. Math was not my best thing, and even worse, I missed the first few weeks of my last year of high school because I had somehow contracted mononucleosis in the last week of summer before school started. This was the year I had registered for two math courses. I was behind the eight ball before the year even started. I worked really hard all year, but was constantly sick because *mono* all but destroyed my immune system.

Since there was no money available for me to go to university, and because I was just barely passing my two math courses, I decided to scrap the university idea. My average wasn't going to be high enough because of the math courses. My parents didn't encourage nor help me. In hindsight, I should have just bailed on that first term, and gone to a different school starting in January—a school which had semesters rather than terms—so I could start over. But since I was generally invisible, nobody suggested that, and I didn't know enough about how things worked to come up with that idea myself. I struggled and gave up on the university idea.

Instead, I applied to the local community college for business administration. I reasoned I could live at home for free. Also, I had been working and saving my money, and had enough to pay cash for my tuition and books. And I had a car. I decided that since things with Rob were clearly stagnant, I could start over with new focus and make some new friends. Friends who didn't know that I was really a *less than, not enough, waste of time, no one will ever want you* loser. I figured doing these things would help me to be strong enough to say *no* to Rob the next time he broke up with me and wanted to get back together.

I was right. One day in September, I came out of my community college to find a note from Rob on my windshield. I knew his handwriting and my heart jumped when I saw it. Carefully, I opened the card. There was a cute cartoon alligator on the front swimming away. Inside, the card just said, "good-bye." That was the straw that broke the camel's back. Now I was being dumped by a card?!

Something happened to me that day. My college wasn't far from Rob's house. It was early afternoon, and as he worked in the restaurant industry, he usually worked evenings. I figured he would be home. I drove to his house and pounded on the door. He answered, and I entered the house. I was so angry I don't even remember what I said, only that I unloaded all the hurt, anger, fear, and rejection I had felt with both barrels. No holds barred. He didn't say a single word. I told him I never wanted to see him again and that I wished I had never met him, or something to that effect. I stormed back out to my car, fired up the engine, and spun the tires on the gravel driveway to further communicate my iron clad decision that I was done with him. Forever.

I was furious. Angry with Rob for continuing to ruin the amazing relationship we had. Angry with myself because I didn't have enough courage or self-respect to stop the downward spiral I found myself in prior to that moment. I had just started my second year of college. I had new friends and did new things with them. I was having fun. I would soon be a college graduate and be able to make something of myself. Without him. So why not start now?

I drove like a maniac but mercifully arrived home safe. When I went to my room, I gathered his gifts—he was an artist, and had given me some very lovely pieces he had made—and threw them all out, save for a few. I threw out all his letters. It all went into a box and straight to the garbage. Despite my anger, I had enough sense to keep the jewellery Rob had given me. For some reason I also kept the photo album that included only pictures of us. Then I sat in my room and cried. No more would I allow myself to be treated like a *less than, not enough, waste of time, no one will ever want you* loser.

I don't recall how much time had passed—a month or so I suppose. I was at home one afternoon with my friend from college, Kim. College classes finished early that day, so Kim and I were hanging out and doing some homework. Rob's car pulled into the driveway. I guess he thought I would be alone because it was early afternoon, my parents were at work, and my car was there. My heart was pounding and I was so grateful that Kim was there. She said nothing, but just having her there gave me the courage to stand my ground and not get sucked back into the emotional hole I was trying to climb out of. I answered the door with the demeanor of a storm cloud. He could see I was there with a friend. He said he wanted to give me my house key back. So, I took the key and slammed the door in his face.

That was a seriously convoluted emotional moment. I felt like a jerk for slamming the door in his face. I didn't want to discuss things with him with Kim there, and I didn't want to get sucked into agreeing to meet with him later. I knew if I did that I probably would not be able to refuse if he asked about getting back together. I just needed him to leave me alone so I could get on with my life. That moment was my chance to keep some distance between us, which I hoped would make it easier to say no to him the next time, if there was a next time. I also didn't want Kim to see me being pathetic by not standing my ground. I felt proud of myself for being able to keep my distance, even if my approach wasn't great. The whole thing left me rather shaken.

Over the next while I sometimes heard him drive by my house in the evenings after he finished work. I had such mixed feelings. I had loved him so much, and yet I felt so deeply hurt. I was heartbroken and confused about what had happened to our relationship. Anyway, no use crying over spilled milk, I thought. I had new friends, a new job, and a car now. I was also a college student, and I was going to soon be a college graduate, get myself a job in the big city, and move away from that wretched place. Interestingly, mother had stopped giving me grief. That was awesome, because I was struggling to keep it together as it was, never mind having to put up with whatever dysfunction she was handing out.

As for giving thanks in all circumstances as 1 Thess 5:18 tells us to do, I was thankful despite the situation being emotionally charged. I was thankful for Kim's presence, which helped me to do *something* that felt true to what I wanted for myself, which was to be in control of myself. To *know* what I wanted, or didn't want, and not be at the whim or mercy of others.

BEGINNING AGAIN

"And we know that in all things God works for the good of those who love Him" (Romans 8:28a NIV).

I eventually met another guy while hanging out with my new friends. He had also worked at my McDonald's, and he was also older than me. He remembered me, and that I was Rob's girlfriend. I remembered his girlfriend as well. Neither of us were dating those people anymore. Eric asked me for my number, and I gave it to him. He called and invited me out with a group of people who were going to celebrate his friend's birthday. I said I would go. We had a fun time. Eric was brave, confident, and exciting. I was captivated.

We began to see more of each other. We went out a lot and I met many of his friends. Eric played competitive sports when he was growing up and got to travel with his various sports teams. He had lots of interesting experiences and was a great storyteller. He didn't seem to be afraid of anything, and did what he wanted to do without caring about people's opinions. I think he enjoyed being a bit outrageous, as it would get a rise out of people, which he found most amusing. We decided to see each other exclusively. All the while, Rob was still driving by my house from time to time. I couldn't begin to understand his intentions.

My time at college was soon to be finished. There was a college teacher's strike, so we had no graduation party/prom. I didn't like my high school prom because Rob and I were broken up at the time, so I went with a friend. I did not have a nice time.

Now I didn't get to have a college prom either. Feeling disappointed and unwilling to let the moment pass unnoticed, my friend and I decided to dress up and go to a fancy restaurant for a steak dinner to celebrate our graduation. The day of this dinner, Rob showed up at my house with a graduation gift for me. It was a very beautiful, breathtaking Cross pen and pencil set. They were matte black with gold trim. I thanked him very much for the gift and then told him to leave. He looked distraught. *Nothing* he could say or do would convince me to put myself in the position of being jerked around by him ever again. It was all I could do to walk away, but I did it. Besides, I had a new boyfriend—one who loved me.

The economy was poor when I graduated from college in 1990, and jobs were hard to come by. I was 21 then, and worked temporary jobs, in addition to the part time job I had at the jewellery store while I was in college. This was not getting a good job in the big city and moving away, but at least I could live in my parent's house for free, work my piddly jobs, save some money, and be with Eric and my friends. Eric was 24. He was a licensed plumber and had a great job. He had a 1964 Comet convertible, which he restored himself, and we would go to car shows and cruise nights to look at the nice old cars and listen to the happy music of the 1950's.

Eric and his friend Ray played hockey together in an industrial league. One Sunday afternoon at their game, Eric had crashed to the ice for some reason, and another player landed on him, dislocating Eric's knee. As I understood it, the knee joint attached the thigh bone and shin bone. The dislocation of Eric's knee made it look like he had two knees on that leg. The joint attaching his thigh bone and shin bone was not doing its job. He was tough, but when he didn't get up off the ice by himself, I knew there was a problem. We took him to the hospital and after what seemed like an eternity, the doctor came.

Eric was on a hospital bed with side rails, and both rails were up. To reset Eric's knee, the doctor had to put the shin bone back into the knee joint. As he did his work, Eric grabbed both bed rails and pushed out on both of them. I couldn't begin to imagine his pain. Eric never made a sound, but both bed rails were bent and would no longer go down. Once Eric's leg was back together, the doctor installed a cast that went from Eric's hip to his ankle. Eric was to be off work for six weeks.

Eric was very exciting and fun. His friend Ray was married to a woman named Leslie. Eric had been friends with them for years. Eric and Ray decided to plan a fun evening for the four of us. They had booked a lovely evening with a multi-course meal at a local high-end restaurant. The meal was to be served in a private room, and we were to be shuttled to and fro via limousine. The catch was, Leslie and I didn't know what was going on. The guys just said to be dressed nicely for May 4, at 5:00 pm. We asked countless questions to try and figure out what was going on, and the guys gave us cryptic answers, which only made us more curious. The event was several months away, so we had plenty of time to drive ourselves into a frenzy trying to figure out what was going on, much to the delight of the guys. They just kept referring to the upcoming event as a "scheme," purposely speaking about it to Leslie and me in a misleading way and chuckling to themselves when we thought we figured out what they were doing.

To make matters more interesting, our "scheme" night was to take place a couple of weeks after Eric's hockey accident, which meant that Eric's pants wouldn't fit. Leslie was a seamstress and sewed him a pair of dress pants with one regular sized leg, and one leg wide enough to accommodate the cast.

Scheme night finally came. We were all at Eric's parent's house, as that was the meeting point. Clearly his parents were in on the scheme, because the formal dining room was set up with the formal dishes. Each fine-china plate had an empty Styrofoam McDonald's box on the plate, which was how burgers were packaged in the early 1990's. We all had a glass of champagne. Unbeknownst to the guys, Leslie and I eventually figured out their scheme. We were going to plan a counter scheme and had come across the very restaurant with the multi-course meal and limo service to and from the event. We thought that seemed quite fun and had decided to book that for the fall. Leslie and I pretended to be seriously disappointed that we had been marinating on "what could this scheme be?!" for months, only to be presented with McDonald's at Eric's parent's house. Leslie and I agreed that we would never tell the guys we had figured out what they were doing, as they were so pleased with themselves for stringing us along on a wild goose chase for several months.

The limo arrived, and we boarded for the 30-minute ride to the restaurant, enjoyed our multi-course meal, and the limo ride home. I laugh at the pictures of that event with Eric's crutches in the background. I suppose the crutches and custom fit pants made the event even more memorable.

That scheme night is one of my fondest memories. From the misleading trail of breadcrumbs to the special pants, to us figuring out what the scheme was and still letting them string us along, to the lovely fun we had on the evening itself, it was an evening to remember. Glitches in the plan was a theme in my life, as I suppose it is in everyone's life. I chose to see the glitches as things that made the event memorable, rather than feeling sour about things being less than perfect.

I knew that Eric had been engaged to be married before, but the girl cheated on him. I kind of understood that. At least Rob just dumped me repeatedly and didn't actually cheat on me, as I chose to believe. Either way, we talked about getting married many times, but I did understand he was "once bitten, twice shy." We had been together for a couple of years by this time and one hot summer night in August, we had a fantastically wonderful fun time at a 50's dance and car show. Eric knew how to swing dance and tried to teach me. I had two left feet but did my best to keep up. Eric seemed to know how to do everything. I was crazy about him. And that night, after dancing the night away, Eric asked me to marry him. He said he had already spoken to my parents about it and they had given their blessing.

That night, I was no longer Eric's girlfriend—I was his fiance. I was beyond thrilled. Eric loved me and believed in me. He encouraged me to do things I had never done before. I no longer felt like a *less than, not enough, waste of time, no one will ever want you* loser. I was going to be somebody's wife.

Romans 8:28 is a very popular verse, that God can work all things for good for those who love him. The day I became Eric's fiancé seemed pretty good to me! By the time I had been with Rob for two years, we had broken up for the first time. By the time I had been with Eric for two years, our relationship was getting better, with the added commitment of being together for the rest of our lives. Eric had a very strong personality and I learned a lot from him about standing up for what you want and what you believe in. Even though Rob and I had a turbulent relationship for two years after the original wonderful two that we were together, I learned that I didn't like myself when I would pretend to be content, and fail to communicate what I wanted and didn't want. It was good that I went through all that with Rob, because it helped me understand that weak point that needed work. Eric being strong in that area provided a model of authenticity. Being aware of that weakness, which was Eric's strength, helped me to embrace a life of being clear on what I want and don't want, becoming a teacher to show me the way, and a man I would spend the rest of my life with.

PRESSING ON

**"But one thing I do: forgetting the past
and what lies behind and straining toward
what is ahead" (Phil 3:13b NIV).**

My engagement ring was beautiful. It was a simple solitaire, which I loved because it was timeless. It would always be simple and beautiful, and never look dated. We were savouring the wonder of our relationship and what our vision for our future looked like, and had not yet settled on a wedding date.

I had acquired a business administration job at a giftware supply company. No more juggling a part time job with crummy temporary jobs. It wasn't a great job, but it was a full time job. The best part was that I worked in the same building as one of the general contractors Eric dealt with, so when he went to their office to discuss drawings or whatever, he would drop in to see me. It was always such a welcome surprise to see him during the work day.

A week after I was seen by Eric's family wearing an engagement ring, Eric's younger sister Tina announced she and her longtime boyfriend were getting married. They had the church and the hall booked for the following August. However, she did not have an engagement ring. Tina's cousin

Tabitha was to be married in June of the following year, which we had all known about for several months. With two weddings in the family within three months of each other, Eric and I decided not to tax the extended family further by adding a third wedding to that summer, so we opted to get married the following year.

I had always wanted to be married in September—the days are warm but not scorching, and in late September the leaves are changing colour in this part of the world, which makes for lovely photographs. The colour scheme could be red. But September was hunting season. We couldn't possibly be married during hunting season because the extended family wouldn't be able to come to the wedding. I wasn't sure how that was a problem, but yet again here we were trying to graciously accommodate everyone but ourselves. We opted for May, in two years. I still went with red for bridesmaid's dresses.

Tina's wedding came and went, and plans for our wedding began to take shape. We learned many things from Tina's planning process. Tina's husband's family was not as affluent as Tina's, and Tina's mother and my mother in law, Joan, brashly told people how much they did for Tina's wedding and how little Tina's husband's family did. I was in the same boat, as my family wasn't as affluent as Tina and Eric's, so we decided that whatever my parents offered to contribute to our wedding, if anything, would be equally matched by Eric's family so we wouldn't have that same kind of bashing going on.

Tina became pregnant on her wedding night, or shortly after, and her baby was due two weeks before our wedding. That was fine, except that she was in our wedding party. Interestingly, she had reamed me out for changing my hairstyle several months prior to her wedding, saying I should have checked with her before I did that. I wasn't sure how I needed her permission to get my hair done. We told her if she felt she had to bow out of being in our wedding that was perfectly fine (actually preferable) but she insisted on being in the wedding. She had her hair redone as well, and didn't check with me first, even though I wouldn't have expected her to. The "do as I say, not as I do" culture was becoming more prevalent. Tina had a videographer at her wedding, and Joan insisted we have one as well. We wanted a unique wedding, not a clone of Tina's. That is probably part of the reason why Eric didn't get along with Tina—even as children. There was an angry, competitive undercurrent as far as they were concerned. Tina appeared to be the parents' favourite because she conformed to their will, while Eric liked to do things his way. That caused a lot of tension, but I loved that about Eric. My mother was also very controlling, so I found it refreshing and amazing that a person could forge their own way and not allow others to control them.

In February of the year I was to marry Eric, specifically on Valentines Day, Rob called my place of work. He said he had called my parents' house and my dad gave him my work phone number. I had no idea why my dad would do that. I wasn't living with my parents anymore, so while I wasn't very impressed that Rob had tracked me down, at least my dad didn't tell him my address or home phone number. Rob called because he wanted to meet me for lunch. On Valentine's Day? I was still angry with him about everything, so I was mean when I told him I would absolutely *not* meet him for lunch, and that I was getting married in a few months. I don't recall how the conversation ended, but I was quite rattled that he was still trying to connect with me four years after we broke up. I don't remember if I told Eric about Rob contacting me or not.

In the coming months, I developed a strong feeling against marrying Eric. Everything was in place—we only had about six weeks to go. Why was I questioning our upcoming marriage? There was one issue on which we agreed to disagree. Maybe it was just cold feet. Maybe it was because I had been thinking about recent happenings with Rob. I reasoned that Eric and I loved each other—surely everything would be fine. I didn't discuss my conundrum with anyone—it was probably just fear. I didn't like being the centre of attention, but as a bride, you are the centre of attention. I also didn't like being photographed, especially since my dad told me that I wasn't as strikingly beautiful as my sister. However, I didn't want fear to control my decision making process like it did when I missed out on going to Calgary, so I just carried on with the plans.

Our wedding day in May of 1992 finally arrived. It was raining that day. I think it rained every weekend that summer. Tina's baby was born two weeks before our wedding, and she was part of the wedding even though we would have preferred it if she bowed out. I don't know how she managed it, but she did. Our photographer was amazing and the rain actually made for beautiful photographs. The camera didn't see the rain, as he put it. There was no wind, and nobody was squinting in bright sunshine. There is a picture of me and my maid of honour under an umbrella, with her fixing my lipstick, which was fun as it wasn't posed. One of the things I loved most about our wedding photographs was all the classic cars. Eric had his 1964 Comet Convertible, and Eric's father, Earl, had purchased a couple of classic cars as well. I believe we had a 1957 T Bird, a 1960 T Bird, and Rolls Royce of a similar vintage for our wedding parade. The Rolls belonged to a friend of Earl's, and that was the "wedding car" that Eric and I rode in, rather than a limousine. It was white and had a beautiful wooden dashboard and steering wheel. With all the rain that year, everything was very green and the park where we had the pictures taken had some nice gravel pathways. The pictures were all very striking.

After the actual wedding ceremony in the church and the photographs in the park, we were on to our wedding dinner. Tina's wedding dinner had been in a super fancy hall, but the food seemed like heated up frozen vegetables and breaded meat products from M&M's, a frozen boxed food company. We wanted our guests to have delicious food, so we booked our dinner at a German Hall. It wasn't fancy, but the food was amazing! Funny how I've always been more about function than appearance. Who cares what it looks like if it doesn't work?

We had a lovely honeymoon in Venezuela—the cheapest trip in the book. Our "honeymoon suite" had two single beds, which made us laugh out loud. Those two single beds in the honeymoon suite were another example of choosing to be happy when things didn't go as I had hoped. It was a lesson that would serve me well in the future. We enjoyed the beach and our first days together as husband and wife. Eric was not one to sit still, so he befriended some people from England who were also vacationing there. He played bocce ball with them a fair bit, and I was happy to sit on the beach and read. The plants in Venezuela were huge. One plant had such huge leaves we could hold the leaf up to our bodies and it would cover an entire torso, which we found funny. So we took a picture. Later that year, a radio station we listened to was having a contest. People were to send in pictures of themselves in their pajamas, and the winners got to go to a comedy club in some pajamas produced by the radio station, stay overnight at a hotel, and go home the next day. We sent in our leaf picture and won a seat at the radio station pajama party. The radio station pajamas were very silly, with fake trap doors on the rear end. That was a fun event.

As Eric and I started our new life together, I was reminded about forgetting what lies behind, and pressing on to what was ahead. I was out of my parents' house and didn't need to deal with my mother. We purposely moved out of town, about a half hour away from our immediate families, so we could see them fairly easily for family functions but not have to worry about them stopping by to hang out. We wanted to keep them at arm's length and make our own way. A fresh start. I was looking forward to it.

GROWING UP – FOR
REAL THIS TIME

**"I can do everything through him who
gives me strength" (Phil 4:13 NIV).**

Eric and I had a lovely little two bedroom house in Two Rivers, a town about 30 minutes south of where we grew up. This was the same town Rob and I had attempted to ride our bicycles to when mine had broken down. We both wanted some distance from our families as we both felt like the "black sheep." Our house was brand new, and no one had lived there. The day we went to look at it, we peeked in all the windows. It was a raised bungalow, so some of the windows were too high to look in without a boost. Eric put me on his shoulders and we went around the house looking in all the windows we could, giggling and laughing the whole time. The builder had built it for someone else and the deal had fallen through for some reason. We contacted him right away, and began the process of buying our first house.

The basement was unfinished, but Eric loved that because he could finish it the way he wanted. He seemed to know how to do everything. On the weekends, he worked away in the basement while I tried new recipes in the kitchen. We were commuters, and we moved in at the end of November, so it was hard to get to know people in town. We decided to join the local curling club in an effort to remedy that. I had been to a curling event through my workplace and it was fun. Neither of us had ever curled before, except for my one-day work event, so the following winter we signed up and had some lessons. Every weekend from October to April, we were curling and meeting new people, and making our house a home.

That winter, my sister gave me an odd birthday gift. She was a teenager then, and her gift was a large chocolate disc, the size of a dessert plate. The accompanying greeting card said something like, "Here is a PMS pill to help you, because you are such a bitch." What? I was shocked and hurt and had no idea what had happened between us that had left her feeling so adversarial towards me, to the point of telling me she thinks I'm a bitch, on my birthday! I was glad to be living a half hour away from this family as the dysfunction my mother dished out appeared to be rubbing off on my sister. In any case, I said nothing. I was simply too shocked to come up with a response of any kind.

Eric began working for his father at the family plumbing business. He was a very hard worker, and with it being a two man shop, and us just starting out, we didn't take vacations except for going to my parents' cottage on the long holiday weekends in the summer. It was really the only place I would have wanted to go anyway, as I loved it there. Eric grew to love it there as well. He helped my dad with various maintenance and upgrade projects around the cottage and talked my parents into letting him cover the roof trusses in the ceiling in the living room with knotty pine boards. They agreed, as long as the existing faux ceiling didn't come down until he was almost finished. They didn't want the cottage being a construction site for the foreseeable future. Eric had to wiggle around in the attic space to get the boards installed. Every time we went to the cottage, he took a load of wood and installed it on the ceiling. It would be a multi-year project. He even bought a boat. It was a zippy little four seater Sea Doo. I was so glad he loved the cottage and enjoyed spending time there as much as I did!

As we became more connected in our community, Eric was invited to play baseball in the summer, and pick-up hockey in the winter. He loved that because he had grown up playing competitive hockey and baseball. He met lots of people who continued to love him no matter what we were doing.

When we moved to Two Rivers, I didn't take my bicycle and really missed it in the summer. One day I came home from work, and Eric had bought me a brand new mountain bike. I was more interested in a road bike than a mountain bike, but I was touched and thrilled that he surprised me with such a thoughtful gift. It was just a department store bicycle, but I loved it anyway. Most mornings that spring, summer, and fall, I would squeeze in a quick ride before I packed up and commuted to my job—a 30 minute drive to another city. Things weren't going very well at the giftware supply company because of the economy, so I applied elsewhere and was hired as a receptionist at an office in the city we grew up in, where Eric's sister Tina worked as an insurance broker.

The insurance office was in a plaza in a subdivision. One day I was leaving work, and who should I see but Rob. He had also been married and was living in that subdivision. His bank was next door to the insurance office where I was working. We exchanged pleasantries. I wasn't sure how I felt about seeing him after all that time.

Time passed, and Eric and I decided to start a family. I wasn't in a hurry to do that, as I knew that would be a life changing event. I was loving my life devoid of dysfunctional treatment from my mother, and enjoying my freedom as a married woman who felt loved. Our baby was due three months before our fifth wedding anniversary. Right around that time, Eric's father decided he didn't want to run the plumbing business anymore, as his friend had just passed away. He probably decided he had worked enough and wanted to enjoy his life, which was totally fair. That happened about a month before the baby was to be born. What would become of Eric's job working for his father if his father was going to close the business? They were a design/build, commercial/industrial plumbing shop. Eric decided to open his own company and continue on.

That meant, however, that it was now a one-man shop, and Eric was that man. This meant he could not take any time off when the baby was born. He was there for the birth, but everything else was business as usual for him. I had never done particularly well with children, and was terrified to be home alone in the winter with this baby. I was also taking a correspondence course for my work, had changed jobs to become an insurance broker myself, and was studying for a designation. Since I didn't get to go to university, having any kind of letters behind my name was meaningful for me. I had one course left to complete the program and obtain my designation. I thought it would be easier to do that while on maternity leave than to try and manage after I had gone back to work. In those days in this part of the world, I could be off for six months with pay. I stretched it to seven months, using vacation time and a bit of unpaid time so I didn't have to go back until September. I got to have the summer off! Summer is my favourite, so I didn't mind having a bit of unpaid time. I sure hated that course, but I also hated being a receptionist. At least as an insurance broker I was licensed for something and was one step up from the bottom as far as office hierarchy is concerned. Not exactly what I had in mind when I graduated from college, but I was happy to have a job.

The baby, our beautiful son Greg, cried from about four in the afternoon to eleven at night, every night, starting when he was about a month old. The good news was that he slept all night. The first time he slept through the night I was afraid he was dead. I figured there must have been something wrong that made him cry the evening before. The evenings weren't fun, but he did sleep all night, which meant I slept all night. I did the course during the day while he napped.

Summer was a busy time for Eric at work. I was home, so I did everything—cooking, cleaning, shopping, laundry, yard work. I wanted him to be able to just come home and be with our son and me, and not have to bother about anything else.

The year our first son was born, the obstetricians in the area were on some kind of strike and were not taking new patients. Greg was born in February, and the strike started some time during my pregnancy, so then I had an obstetrician. My friend was expecting her first baby in June, and she did not have an obstetrician. That would have been ok, except that she had toxemia. Her family doctor just told her to take it easy. Well, she had a desk job, so that was pretty easy, right? My friend ended up in the hospital. The obstetrician who cared for me and delivered my baby was working at the hospital when my friend went in. She was induced, and gave birth to a beautiful baby girl, but the baby died 18 hours after she was born. My friend and her husband were devastated.

I was beside myself with guilt and fear. My friend and her husband were Christians, and they helped with the youth group at their church. I grew up in the church, but had turned my back on it. The "Christianity" of my mother left me feeling like none of that was real. The shame I felt about how she treated me and how I pretended everything was fine. I figured it was my fault that she was awful to me, and how could God let me be born into that? Well, a whole new level of shame rose up in me. How could God let my friend's baby die, when she was faithful? I thought it should be *my* baby that died because I wasn't faithful. That would serve me right.

The funeral was devastating. My friend's baby looked like a china doll in a shoe box, but the way my friend and her husband trusted God through that experience deeply moved me. I wanted that kind of faith. The kind of faith that could trust God even in the midst of unspeakable pain. It would be easy for something like that to destroy the marriage as well, but it only brought them closer together. I was inspired to go back to church. Eric and I discussed it, and we decided to try the local Presbyterian church. His mother had taken him to Presbyterian church as a child, so that was what he knew. That was good enough for me, so off we went to Presbyterian church. The church I grew up in seemed like it was more about rules regarding all the things you couldn't do, so I was happy to try something else. I wanted to *know* God and feel close to Him, like my friends did. I wasn't sure the church I grew up in could deliver that.

In those days, the church times were published in the newspaper. The paper said the service started at 11:00 am, but that was an older paper. The service started at 10:00 am in the summer. The Sunday we arrived was the first Sunday in July, and the service ended shortly after we arrived, with our baby in tow. Shirley, the retired kindergarten teacher who was the nursery coordinator at the church, introduced herself, took us on a tour of the church and the nursery, then introduced us to the minister. I was blown away by how friendly and kind the people were. And so began our journey back to God.

The minister and his wife were the most lovely people I had ever met. They were in their early 60's, so they were a bit older than my parents. Sheryl, the minister's wife, invited me to be part of a ladies group called "Hands in Praise." They did sign language to songs. I decided to accept her invitation as it was another opportunity to get involved in the community and meet people. We met at Sheryl's house once a week, and worked together with our American Sign Language dictionaries to select signs that flowed with the music. I loved that group. I really enjoyed music, and to add another element, the signing, gave it a real depth. It was also wonderful to get to know Sheryl and the other ladies. I especially loved Sheryl, because she was like a mother to me. She had four adult children, and was the best mom ever. I wished I had a mom like her. Her husband John, the minister, was an absolutely delightful man. He was very intelligent and educated, and knew how to do everything. Eric and I became friends with John and Sheryl. When Eric needed an authorized signature for his work—completing a job or something—John was qualified to do that signing, so Eric would go and visit with him and get his documents signed.

That September, I went back to work. I worked out of town, so it was about a 45 minute drive to my workplace. It was challenging to leave my seven month old son with a babysitter. I wanted to be home with him, but I also wanted to make a financial contribution to the home. I left at 8:00 am, and by the time I picked the baby up and got home, it was 6:00 pm. I would make supper and put the baby to bed, clean up, get ready for the next day, and start all over again. I decided to hire a cleaning lady who came every Friday, so my house was clean for the weekend and I could just be with my son. Eric worked late every night, except the nights he was curling. I had a very hard time managing, as the job I went back to was a promotion of sorts, and I had no training on how to do the job. I felt completely incompetent everywhere I went. It was awful. Going back to work was not great—after paying the babysitter and the cleaning lady, there wasn't much money left.

In time, I learned my new job and felt competent at work. I developed processes at home to do things more efficiently so I could manage the cleaning myself, even though I appreciated the cleaning lady and her work, and would have loved to have kept her. And of course the baby was growing, so he could walk and feed himself a little bit, which also helped.

Just as I was beginning to get the hang of things, I slipped going up the stairs one Sunday in January and broke my right foot. Greg was about a year old, and had been walking for a couple of months. He rapidly progressed to running everywhere. Needless to say, taking care of a wild, running year old boy was next to impossible with a broken foot. My work wanted me back ASAP, and since I could not drive, they arranged for me to ride in with a new hire who lived sort of near me. Being on crutches in Canada in February was tricky. Mercifully, I did not fall on any ice and we all survived the six weeks of carpooling while my foot was in a cast.

Life carried on, and in time we decided to have another baby. Around Easter of the following year, I was almost three months pregnant, and we hadn't told anyone about the pregnancy yet. Eric's brother, Seth, had decided to abandon his career, become a plumber, and join Eric in running his new plumbing company. When Seth announced at Easter that he and his girlfriend were getting married, Eric took him aside and said that we were expecting a baby in November, and trusted that their wedding would be at a different time than our baby was due. Unfortunately, their wedding was planned for that November, the same weekend that our second baby was due. Eric was there the day of the birth, but that was it. He was running his company while his brother was on honeymoon, and I was home by myself with a newborn son, Kyle, and an active, intelligent two year old. In the winter. In Canada. I was frustrated that this was my second baby, and the second time that Eric was unable to be with me after bringing our new baby home. I also felt very selfish for wanting Eric to be with me. I knew how important Seth's wedding and honeymoon was, but out of the whole year, did it have to be that week?

I then remembered the day my mother grabbed me by the shoulders and started banging me against the wall because I asked why I couldn't have my friend for a sleepover. She told me I was a "selfish rotten kid." Here I was again, feeling selfish and rotten because I was frustrated that other people's needs trumped my own. Did my needs matter to anyone? I didn't want people to feel like I felt when called selfish and rotten. I didn't want to *be* selfish and rotten, or perceived as selfish and rotten. So, like the day my mother abandoned me at the mall, I didn't say anything. I didn't want to ask my mother for help. I grew up feeling like an inconvenience to her, and even at 30,

I was still treated like an inconvenience. I just struggled on the best I could. My grandmother had six children, a six-hole wood stove on which to cook and warm the kitchen, and she didn't drive. My grandfather was a minister, so they had little money. Whatever I was dealing with was nothing compared to what my grandmother dealt with, and she was the most lovely, peaceful, patient, kind, and competent person I knew. Grandma was from Arizona, so her family was far away. They had moved to northern Ontario, so even my grandfather's family was far away. They didn't have family to help them either. If grandma could manage, so could I.

Eric and I decided that I would stay home with the two boys. By then, he was well established with his own company. In contrast, paying for two kids to be in daycare would swallow up the majority of my paycheque, so it didn't make much sense for me to go back to work. I did, however, want a dishwasher. Our little house didn't have one. Eric was working all the time and I did all the dishes. I thought with the two boys, a dishwasher would help me manage the growing workload. He disagreed. This time, however, I decided to meet my need and purchased a dishwasher with the money I earned and had it installed. It felt really good to know what I wanted and make it happen for myself. Eric never spoke about the dishwasher. I realized I had power, and I stood in that power. I was also glad that standing in my power did not cause an argument with Eric.

I was enjoying my new relationship with God, as opposed to the rules-based "relationship" I had with Him growing up. The dishwasher event was a trivial thing, but it was interesting to me how I was able to stand up for myself and be strong enough to make something happen for myself. If I could do that, what else could I do with God's strength, as it says in Philippians 4:13?

THE SWEET SPOT

"For my yoke is easy and my burden is light" (Matt 11:30 NIV).

I loved being home with the boys. Greg was wonderful with baby Kyle—he was a great big brother. The boys became really good buddies, and being with them as they grew was such a blessing to me. One of the other ladies in Sheryl's "Hands in Praise" group, Sarah, was my age and had a son Greg's age. Sarah and her family had lived in Two Rivers all their life, so she was well connected. She and I decided to start a Bible study, which we held at my house. There were four of us, three of whom had a child in junior kindergarten. The kids were at school all day Monday, Wednesday, and every other Friday, as they all had the same schedule. We had the Bible study at my house because I still had Kyle at home. We did our meeting in the afternoon when Kyle had his nap and the others were at school. It was wonderful to develop friendships with such lovely people, and to grow in our faith at the same time.

We continued to spend our long summertime weekends at the cottage with the boys. As the boys grew, they grew to love it there as well. They were the fourth generation to go to that cottage and I was grateful to my other grandfather for building this fabulous place. It was like a piece of heaven to me.

At home, there was construction in a nearby neighbourhood, with large construction machines everywhere. I would put the boys in the wagon and bring a backpack full of snacks and drinks. They would sit in the wagon and watch the machines for a good long time. Then they would have their snack and we would go home. Sarah gave me a trailer that she was no longer using to go with my bicycle, and I bought a bicycle for Greg. He was all fired up with his training wheels, and with baby Kyle in the bike trailer, we would ride around the neighbourhood. I was so thankful for my bicycle and that I could ride with my sons. I wondered if that was how my father had felt those times when he bought bicycles for me and taught me how to ride.

I had the boys in swimming lessons at the local YMCA. Eric grew up playing ice hockey, and the local arena had a "learn to skate" program on Saturday mornings which cost $2 for the whole season. There was also free ice time on Tuesday and Thursday mornings, so I laced Greg up and he would skate to his heart's desire while I followed behind with Kyle in the stroller.

We also did crafts and baking. The library had a story hour, so Greg would go to that, do crafts, and hear a story, and I would choose books to read to the boys at bedtime. I loved having them both on my lap, all snuggly with their soft little boy hair, reading books that we had just discovered, along with favourites from my childhood. We discovered "Mighty Machines" videos for kids, with footage of machines working and commentary on what they were doing. Kyle loved the one about the garbage truck. On the days when Greg was in kindergarten, Kyle liked to follow the garbage man, so I would bundle him up and outside we would go. He watched the garbage men load the truck, have the crusher crush the garbage, and drive on to the next house. We followed along. One spring day, the garbage man gave Kyle a brand new kite. I have always appreciated the garbage man and hope that the interest my little boy showed in his work was meaningful to him.

That spring, Eric went to a conference on in-floor heating. It was out of town, and he was gone for about five days between the conference and the travelling. I was alone with the boys for that time, and on Sunday, I helped in the church nursery as I thought it would be fair to take a turn caring for my child and the other toddlers there. While Eric was gone, I was counting down to his return. I missed him so much and was afraid I couldn't manage without him. At least it was only a few days. He surprised me by coming home early, coming to the church nursery directly from the airport. I was overjoyed to see him. He was a great dad and I loved watching him play with the boys.

I continued to handle everything at home, which was fine, because I was home and not making a financial contribution. My contribution was to make the house a home Eric could return to after work, have a hot meal, and play with his sons.

Sometimes Eric would invite me and the boys to a jobsite he was working on to see the equipment. At one site he gave Greg a scissor lift ride. At another, he had a bulldozer ride. Kyle was a bit too young for that still, but Greg loved it. I spent much of my childhood being afraid and hiding in my room. My dad did the best he could by helping me with my bicycles. One time, when I was sick, he bought me some playdough and I heard my mother yelling at him because of the play dough mess she would have to clean up. My dad wanted to do nice things, but it usually caused problems for him. It was wonderful to see my husband enjoying his sons and showing them fascinating things, and it was wonderful for me to be part of it and allow the relationship between them and their dad to flourish.

I really loved being home with the boys, watching them learn and grow. They shared the other bedroom in our two-bedroom house. Eric had finished the basement and it was awesome. There was a large rec room with a gas fireplace, which was super cozy on cold, dark winter nights. One Saturday night, Eric and I were watching a movie downstairs when we heard some noise upstairs. What on earth was going on? I creeped up the stairs and I was able to peek into the boys' room from my vantage point on the stairs. Greg was in a bed, but Kyle was still in the crib. After I had read them some stories, tucked them in, and left the room, Greg was going across the room to Kyle's crib, making noise or faces or something, and Kyle was laughing hysterically. When the laughing started, Greg dove back into his bed. What a hoot! I loved that the boys were such good buddies.

Lynn, the lady who babysat Greg when I went back to work, had four sons. Eric knew her husband from work. He was an electrical contractor and they often worked on the same jobs. Lynn did home daycare. That was a wild, fun house. Eric and I were enjoying our sons, and loved all the stories Lynn and her husband told us about theirs. We decided to have another baby, and this meant that we would need a bigger house. Eric had built a large deck in the large back yard, so the boys would have a wonderful place to play away from the road. We also lived next to a park, so playground equipment was very close by. Still, I really appreciated having my own bedroom when I was growing up, so I wanted that for my sons as well. Eric's construction business was very successful, and we had been living in our little house for almost ten years.

Around the time I began to suspect I was pregnant, I was on my way to take the boys to another jobsite, as Eric had arranged for them to check out a backhoe. There was no one there that day except the backhoe operator and Eric. On the drive to the jobsite, I heard on the radio about the twin towers being hit. At first, I thought it was an accident. I wondered how in the world an airplane could fly into a building. Then it happened again. And something hit the Pentagon. What in the world was going on?

I didn't immediately understand what had happened, but arrived at the jobsite. Eric took the boys to the backhoe, and the operator showed Greg how to work the controls. Greg spent some time digging in the ditch the operator had already started. I will forever remember September 11, 2001. Here I was, having a wonderful life with my husband and my beautiful sons, while other people's husbands were killed in a terrorist attack. I was so grateful to God for the wonderful life I was having. I later learned that over 50 of the men killed in those attacks had a pregnant wife at home. My heart went out to them.

Later that fall, the church decided to put on an Easter play the following spring. Easter was going to be in March in 2002. With Easter coming early, the team wanted to get organized in good time. They asked Eric to play Jesus in the Easter play. He had a real presence about him and was fantastic with little kids. He agreed to do it.

A few months later in the first week of December, as my third pregnancy progressed, we started looking for a new place to call home. A place on the highway into the neighbouring city was for sale. I had always loved that house, so we decided to look at it. We had hired a babysitter to take care of our sons, who were two and four years old then. The showing was on a Saturday morning, and the babysitter didn't show up. That was before cell phones, so we couldn't call the realtor to say we weren't coming. I suggested we just go and bring the boys with us. I offered to wait in the car with the boys if things got out of hand. As "luck" would have it, the people who owned the home were empty nesters, and they had two boys as well. Of course, their boys were grown, but I believe that seeing our two little boys run around the house was very endearing to them.

We *loved* the house. It had three bedrooms, and could easily be renovated to add a fourth. The property also had almost 13 acres, most of that being wooded areas, which would give the boys an awesome place to play. We could store our boat on our own property. Eric put in an offer on the house, and the realtor said that someone else had offered more and they were turned down. Eric stuck to his guns and his offer was accepted. We asked to close the deal at the end of June the following year, when Greg was finished with school for the year, which would mean he wouldn't have to change schools mid year, or need to be driven to school. Also, our baby was due in May, and we figured moving with a baby would be easier than moving while pregnant. It turned out the sellers wanted a long closing date, as they were downsizing and building a new house in town. It was a great deal for all of us.

In Matthew 11:30, Jesus tells us that His yoke is easy and his burden is light. What I got from that verse was trying to do things myself in my own way would be a tough slog. But if

I trusted God and did things His way, and consulted Him on various matters, life would be much easier. Since our active return to church, with me hosting a ladies Bible study in my home, life seemed easy and wonderful. It did seem that doing things God's way and trusting Him day by day was a much better way to live than plowing ahead with my own ideas. Being in relationship with God did not have to be full of rules and shame like I learned growing up. Being in relationship with Him and doing things His way really was easy and light.

THE UNTHINKABLE

"The thing that I feared most is that which has come upon me" (Job 3:25 NIV).

Christmas of 2001 was pretty exciting. We had looked at the house I loved on the highway, and the sellers had accepted our conditional offer. Now we had to list our house for sale. We had prospective buyers going through our house between Christmas and New Year's. We would go to Eric's parents house when the realtor was showing our house to prospective buyers. Eric's parents lived about a half hour away, so it was a bit of a production to pack up the kids and drive to grandma and papa's house. Eric took some time off over the holidays and that helped a lot. One young couple wanted to look at the house ASAP. The realtor called around 6:00 pm while I was making supper and Eric was at work. I told the realtor he could bring the people that day if he wanted to, but I had to stay there with the kids. If everyone was ok with that, then come on over. At the time Greg was four, almost five. The young couple came in and Greg greeted them at the door, proceeding to give them a tour of the house. He was so much like Eric—they could both have a conversation with anyone and make them feel at ease.

In January, the realtor came to us with two offers, and only three people had looked at the house. Another realtor waited in his car while we were presented with the offers. In the end, the young couple Greg gave a tour purchased our little house. I wondered how it felt to them to come into the house, smell food cooking, and have two little boys playing, one of whom gave a guided tour of the house. It was a very cozy home that cold, dark winter evening.

Our buyers were thrilled. This would be their first home, just like it was ours. That was great also because they didn't have any conditions on the offer. They didn't have a house to sell, and had been pre-approved for a mortgage. Just like that, the wheels were in motion for us to move to the fabulous house on the highway in June of 2002.

In February Greg had his fifth birthday. He was in junior kindergarten, so we decided to just invite some of our friends who had kids to come over for a BBQ and have some cake—we all had fun.

By now I was noticeably pregnant. I could feel the baby moving, and I loved that. I loved being pregnant. I loved imagining what this wee person would look like and be like. I felt like I knew them already, because we had spent so much time together before they were even born. It was such a magnificent miracle to give life and I was certain this baby was going to be a boy. Eric and I chose a name together for him.

The winter was mild, and there was a lot of rain and no snow, which was odd for February where we lived. Our usual kids activities of skating on Tuesday and Thursday mornings continued, along with the story hour program at the library. One day, while I was driving to one of our activities, Greg asked me to tell him about the car accidents his dad had been in. It was a very odd question, but Eric had been in a few fender benders. In fact, I had teased Eric that we probably shouldn't have another baby because he had been in a minor accident during both of my other pregnancies, and the second accident was worse than the first. Maybe that was why Greg was asking about the accidents. Maybe he had heard me say that. I will never know for sure.

That night, after the boys had their bath, I read library books with the boys on my lap. I loved that. I tucked them into their beds and went downstairs to watch TV until Eric came home. He worked such long hours. It was past 8:00 pm that Friday evening. By then, Eric had a cell phone. They were fairly new in 2002, but in construction, they were a necessity as there were no phones on the job site. In any case, he had a habit of calling me while on his way home on the days he worked late. He was working about 45 minutes from home at the time, so he was driving on a major highway. We talked for 15 minutes or so, and were disconnected. Cell service wasn't great in 2002, so dropped calls were a common occurrence. He would often call back if the call was dropped. I knew he was about ten minutes from home, so I wasn't concerned when he didn't call back. He would be home in a few minutes anyway, so what would be the point of calling back? Ten minutes turned into an hour, and I began to worry.

The phone rang, but it wasn't Eric. It was Eric's father. He said there had been an accident and he was going to pick me up to take me to the hospital. I called my friend Sarah from my Bible study group and asked her to stay with the boys, and she came right over.

When we got to the hospital, Eric's parents, his siblings and their spouses, and me, all gathered into a little room. The Doctor simply said, "I'm sorry, there's nothing we could do."

Nobody said anything.

Then I said, "Are you telling me that Eric is dead?"

"That's right", the Doctor said.

He died in the ambulance before he made it to the hospital. Nobody knows what happened, but the construction van he was driving hit something and was rolling in the centre ditch on the highway. I guess someone saw that and called 911. It was about 8:30 on that Friday when Eric's van rolled. There wasn't much traffic, so at least it was a single vehicle accident and no-one else was hurt. Eric's wallet with his identification in it was not in his pocket, but in the console somewhere. The hospital called the number on the side of the construction van. The office was in Eric's parents house, so that is how they were involved.

I was absolutely devastated. I was seven months pregnant with our third child. I had a two year old and a five year old. I was an at-home mom and had been for over two years. I was supposed to move to the beautiful house on the highway with Eric, help him with the administration and bookkeeping in his construction business, and raise our kids. How could this be? Eric was 35 years old, four weeks away from his 36th birthday. I had just turned 33 and learned that our next breath is not guaranteed.

I had not been to a funeral until I was in my twenties, and I was shocked by how different a person looked in a casket than they did when vibrantly alive. I was determined to go in and see Eric in the hospital, as I knew he would be almost unrecognizable in a casket. I decided to call Sarah, who was staying with the boys, to let her know what was going on and that I might be gone a while. She must have called John, the minister, because around 10:30 that night, John arrived at the hospital. I told him I wanted to go in and see Eric and was just trying to get prepared for that. John said he would go in with me, and he went in alone first to see what the situation was.

The hospital gave me a wheelchair, presumably because I was seven months pregnant. Pastor John returned from the room where Eric was and brought me in by Eric's side. John stood behind Eric's head. I just sat there and cried and cried. I stood up and threw myself across Eric's body and just cried until I was exhausted. Pastor John waited patiently and wheeled me back out to the waiting room when I was finally finished seeing Eric as himself for the last time.

It was probably midnight when I got home. I thanked Sarah profusely for staying with the boys and for calling Pastor John. She was such a dear friend. At that moment, I knew that starting to attend the Two Rivers church was the smartest thing I'd ever done.

The next day was Saturday. I was supposed to get my hair cut, and Eric and I were to attend a dinner at the men's bonspiel at the curling club. His company was sponsoring the event, so the event organizer had invited us to the dinner. I cancelled my hair appointment and called the event organizer to let him know that we wouldn't be attending because Eric had died the night before in a car accident. The man was devastated—he and Eric were on the board at the curling club and had become great friends.

That day was a whirlwind of activity with people coming and going. How do you tell a five year old his father is dead? Greg had a friend from school whose mother was amazing. She was friends with Sarah, who probably told her about Eric. She called and invited Greg to come and play for the day, which was lovely. She picked him up and dropped him off, and that kept him out of the fray for the day.

The following week, when I went to the funeral home with Eric's family to choose the casket, I burst into tears. People were coming in droves and dropping off food, which I just kept putting in the freezer. It was a most welcome relief to not have to bother about cooking. I was extra grateful for my dishwasher with all that was going on.

Pastor John was at my house what seemed like every day as we put together the funeral service. Eric and I had been enjoying a new band called CREED. The lyrics to some of their songs were so beautiful and perfect. I played the songs for Pastor John and he agreed to have them played at the funeral service. That was really something, as CREED was an alternative rock type of band, and the church was conservative. Eric's childhood friend was living in Capital City at the time, but he came and played the bagpipes at the funeral. The church was packed. *Packed.* I believe the church could hold about 700 people, and it was full.

There were several visitations at the funeral home in the days before the funeral service. They gave me a chair, which was wonderful. I was told there was a lineup outside and people had been waiting for 45 minutes to get in to see Eric's family and me. I really appreciated that, especially since most of those people had probably also driven 45 minutes or more just to get to Two Rivers. It meant so much to me that Eric had meant so much to so many people, and that they took that amount of time to express that to me and his family. I arrived early to one of the visitations and was able to secure a few minutes alone with Eric before people started coming in. Again, I threw myself across his body and cried. How was I ever going to manage without him? I was so broken-hearted and afraid. How could a person hurt this badly and still be able to get up and walk around?

The day of the funeral arrived. My friend Crystal, also from church, offered to take care of Kyle during the funeral. That was most thoughtful and welcome, as I wasn't in a position to deal with a two year old and a five year old that day. Greg came to the funeral. After I spoke to those present, Greg wanted to speak as well, so I picked him up and held him up to the microphone. He said something about his daddy and lots of people started to cry. It was a very emotional experience. I had arranged to have a gentleman from church record the service since the boys were so young, and the baby wasn't born and would never know his father. I thought they might like to see the service some day.

After the service, refreshments were served in the church basement dining room. I saw a woman there I hadn't seen before. She was just leaving and I didn't get a chance to speak with her. With all the people, noise and emotions, it's a wonder I remember anything about that. My mother told me the lady's name was Samantha and that she had been married to my cousin who had died in a car accident the year before. Her kids were six and four at the time.

After the time of refreshments was over, the family went to the cemetery alone. We decided to bury Eric in the town that was between where I lived and where Eric's parents and siblings lived. That seemed like a fine arrangement for everyone. As the family was milling about at the cemetery, the finality of it all suddenly hit me very hard. I was very glad I had seen Eric in the hospital, because in that casket, he really didn't look like himself at all. He had been thrown from the construction van (not wearing his seat belt) and his head was crushed, his jaw broken. He looked so *not* like himself that the events were all closed caskets. I told the funeral director I would like to have some of Eric's hair and the poor gentleman secured some of it for me, which I somehow took home and put in a ziploc bag. People do very odd things when they are drowning in grief and sorrow.

The next odd thing I did, while drowning in my grief and sorrow, was to drive out to the place on the road where Eric's van had rolled. It was the first week of March, and still no snow. I wondered if there were any pieces of debris in the ditch. So there I was, seven months pregnant, crawling around on my hands and knees in the ditch on a divided highway, looking for God knows what. My father-in-law found out about that and learned where Eric's van had been taken. He took me to see that instead of having me go out to the highway again. I gathered Eric's hard hat, his wallet, his Gatorade bottle...it was all so....surreal. The van didn't even look that bad. I had seen accidents where the people walked away unhurt and the vehicle looked way worse than Eric's van. *Why? Why? Why?* What was going to become of me and my precious sons? And my baby?

My mother gave me Samantha's phone number, as I was eager to connect with someone who had a clue about what I was dealing with. She was lovely, shared my faith, and told me about what had happened to her husband. People don't really want to know how you are when they say, "How are you?" You can't tell people how you really are—nobody has that much time. Speaking with Samantha was a gift from God. Someone I could tell how I was actually feeling, who understood, and who was not afraid of my pain, no matter how overpowering it was. We developed a wonderful friendship and visited each other. Her husband had died eight months before mine, so it was also encouraging for me to see that she was OK, or at least better than she had been at her husband's funeral. That did give me some hope that we would make it. Our kids were around the same age, so that was nice for them too.

Of course, there was the matter of the Easter play. All of this happened four weeks before the play. The church and the rest of the people involved in the play had been working on the play since Christmas. Pastor John asked me if I wanted them to cancel the play. I said no, that Eric would want the show to go on. There were two performances—Good Friday, and the Saturday evening between Good Friday and Easter Sunday. They found someone else to play Jesus. One of the Two Rivers parishioners had created a cross that could be raised with a man on it. The play was very well done. The lights were low and when they were "nailing Jesus to the cross," the sound effects were very effective. With each blow of the hammer, I imagined Jesus dying for me, and Eric's van rolling in the ditch.

I went to the Saturday night show on Eric's birthday. There was a cast party at someone's house after the performance and I went to that as well. That was the closest I would get to being with Eric on his birthday.

I couldn't let grief and sorrow destroy me, and I wanted to maintain the routine as much as possible for the boys' sake. God had allowed this to happen, and He promised to never leave me, so we would be OK, somehow. I remembered the Bible story in Daniel about the fiery furnace. Even though the furnace had been ordered to be seven times hotter than usual, God was with them, and when they came out, they didn't even smell like smoke. So I took Greg to school, we continued with the skating and the library story hour, and went to church on Sundays. I did grocery shopping when Greg was in school, so I only had one child to manage at the store. As long as Kyle was pinned down, he was OK. While

Greg was loud and wild, at least I always knew where he was. Kyle was very cerebral, very quiet, and very curious. He was the "silently wander away" type. Since he was still two, I could keep him in the grocery cart and not worry about him disappearing.

The first time I went to get groceries by myself after Eric died, they had cottage cheese on sale. Eric loved cottage cheese, so I burst out crying in the store. That first year was so difficult—I just never knew when I was going to burst out crying because of something that reminded me of Eric. Everything seemed to remind me of Eric. The one CREED song that Pastor John let me play at the funeral was popular on the radio, and I heard it all time, which was oddly comforting somehow. I felt like Eric was with me in some way.

Eric's family began coming regularly to pack up my house, as I still had to move. I signed Greg up for soccer and T ball that year, and my father-in-law faithfully came and took Greg to these activities. We spent a lot of time on the weekends with them too. Eric worked late all the time, and if he wasn't working late, he was curling or at a board meeting or a play practice. For the boys, not having him there during the week wasn't too difficult. The weekends were another story. I remembered the year before when Eric was at a conference and was away for several days. Knowing he would be back helped me to keep going. This time, he wouldn't be back, so I had to find another way to keep going.

When Eric and I were married, I was 23 and he was 26. He died about three months before our tenth wedding anniversary. The year we were married, he had arranged for us to have life insurance and wills, which was very cost effective since we were so young and had nothing to leave to anyone.

So the wills read that if he died, I got everything he owned, and vice versa. Because he had owned property before, he didn't qualify for the government Home Ownership Savings Plan. It was a government grant of sorts, so we put the house in my name in order to take advantage of the grant. Other than that I didn't own anything to leave him. By the time Eric died, he was part owner of his construction business, so I became the president. That was ridiculous as I didn't know anything about construction. The lawyers did their bit, and Eric's brother bought out my share of the business. Between that and the life insurance, I would be OK as far as finances were concerned.

I had always been afraid that Eric would die, and now he was dead. In Job 3:25, the Bible says, "What I feared has come upon me; what I dreaded has happened to me." Of course, Job had it way worse than I did at that moment, but my life wasn't exactly going according to plan either.

I remembered being afraid of going to Calgary to visit my aunt and uncle when I was 14. I didn't go and was always sorry about it. Having two situations in my life that were fear based, both producing reprehensible results, gave me pause to think about the wisdom of being afraid. I decided that I would not allow fear to control me again, because I certainly did not want more results like these.

GOOD, BAD, AND UGLY

**"Even though I walk through the valley of
the shadow of death, I will fear no evil, for
you are with me" (Psalm 23:4 NIV).**

One night in the first week of May, my water broke. Of the
three births, the first two were induced. This was the only
one to happen naturally, which was fine, except that I was
the only adult in the house, it was 2:00 am, and my family
was all 30 minutes away. At least there wasn't a lot of traffic
at 2:00 am.

I called Eric's parents, Earl and Joan, and let them know.
My other two deliveries had been very fast. So fast, in fact,
that the obstetrician who had delivered Greg had a student
doctor in the room when Kyle was born to observe. We knew
I might not have much time. I didn't call my parents because
I knew needing that kind of help in the middle of the night
would be off the charts inconvenient for my mother. Earl
and Joan came, and Earl stayed at the house with the boys.
Joan drove me to the hospital. My friend arrived, and so did
Eric's sister. Once the labour really began, my third son was
born about 6:00 am. Although Eric hadn't been able to spend
any time with me after the other two boys had been born,

I would have given anything in that moment to have him there for the birth alone, and not been the least bit bothered if he wasn't able to be home for anything else. Perspective is an interesting thing.

I didn't get to hold my new baby boy right away, because the doctor thought she detected a heart murmur. Some wise advice I received from a friend who separated from her husband and delivered a baby alone was to get a private room at the hospital. Listening to your roommate's husband when you have no one coming is hard. That was great advice. Not only did I not have my husband coming, there was no baby to come and see, as he was being evaluated by the medical staff. Mercifully, I had a private room. I sat in the chair and looked out the window, and had a conversation with God. I said, "Well, God, I have a dead husband, a two year old, a five year old, no job, no skills, and a newborn who potentially has health problems. There is *nothing* I can do here. I need you to show up. If you don't, I'm sunk."

There was no point in worrying, as worry never solves anything. I remembered that strong feeling I felt a few months before I married Eric...that I shouldn't marry him. What if I had listened to that? I might not be in this giant mess. Of course, things might be worse. In any case, I reasoned that God had allowed all of this to happen, so He would need to figure it out. All I could do was get up every day and take care of my sons. If the baby had health problems, then God would have to provide a way to deal with it. I had no other option. When you're in a place so tough that only God can help you, you get to know Him very well.

The baby was born on a Tuesday. I named him Evan, the name Eric and I had chosen together. I was able to see him and the hospital arranged for me to take him to a specialist at a university hospital an hour away on Friday. Earl was at home with Kyle and Greg. I wanted to pick Greg up from school on Wednesday, and I did just that. I just wanted to be home with my precious sons.

On Friday, Greg was in school again. My parents had a mini-van, and took me, the baby, and Kyle to the specialist an hour away. After examining the baby, the doctor concluded that the odd sounding heartbeat was a result of him being born so quickly. As I understood it, there is a flap of skin that covers a part in the heart which hadn't been sealed yet when the attending medical team checked him after he was born. The baby had a clean bill of health! I was deeply and profoundly grateful for that. On the way home from that appointment, Kyle developed a fever. That weekend was Mother's Day, and my friend from college came to the house and wanted to make a meal for me for Mother's day, then clean my house. Kyle's fever turned out to be hand-foot-and-mouth. He was in a bad way, so he slept in the bed with me until I had to get up to nurse the baby. Then my friend stayed in the bed with Kyle. And so began the fast-moving treadmill of being a widow with three sons five years old and under.

Earl told my mother to come and stay with me, so she did. I wonder if that was as hard for her as it was for me. I was in a very bad way, so at least she was nice to me.

Eric's family continued to come and pack my house. My friend's brother, who had moved many times during his tenure as a professional athlete, had offered to organize the move to the new house. In a way I wanted to stay where I was, because that was the home I had with Eric. But it was still a two-bedroom house, now I had three kids, and the deal was done. The only thing to do was move. On the last day of school in June 2002, I took Greg to school, Kyle to daycare, and went to the park. I went to the lawyer's office amongst other things to keep busy for the day. I picked Greg and Kyle up from their respective activities and brought them home to our new house. Both boys had their own room, and the moving team had set up all the bedrooms. There was a table for an electric train set that came with the house, and someone had set up Greg's Thomas the Tank Engine track on that table. He was delighted!

The baby was set up in my room with me. I told Earl I would need some kind of fenced play area because Kyle was known to silently wander and I would struggle to keep track of him with everything else that was going on. We lived on the highway going out of Two Rivers, so the road was busy. The house was far back from the road, but still...

Earl found some cheap horse fence and some posts, and put a team together to put up the fence. The day the fence went up, Earl came into the house and asked if Kyle was inside. I said that he was. Earl was so relieved. Kyle had been outside with the team, and decided to come in the house. Earl didn't see him leave, and he said the team was walking up and down the highway and through the wooded area looking for him. I was sorry they had to go through that, but at least he understood why I wanted the fence!

Shortly after the fence went up, Kyle was playing in the yard. I was keeping an eye on him while I did things in the house. He was walking around outside the fence. What on earth? I just watched to see what he would do. He collected his ball that had gone over the fence, and thrown it back over into the play area. Then he walked around to the gate, and crawled under it back into the yard. I told Earl, and he nailed a board on the bottom of the gate so Kyle wouldn't be able to escape again.

That was our first summer in that house. I had all the boys, all the time, because Greg was no longer in school. Eric had looked into doing martial arts at the dojo by our former house. He had always liked martial arts, and thought it would be something he and Greg could do together. He had met with the owner of the school, Joe, and had brought home a schedule with the classes Greg would go to. That summer, I signed Greg up for a karate day camp in a nearby town. That town was a half hour away, but I could find out if he liked it or not before I signed him up for a regular program near our house. And driving around would give me something to do. Kyle never complained while riding in the car, and the baby just slept.

Greg *loved* martial arts. He even earned his yellow belt that first week at karate camp, and took part in a demonstration. I met with Joe at our local school, explained about Eric meeting him, and the one week of day camp, and that Eric had died after signing Greg up. Joe was *amazing* with Greg. He was probably only 20 years old at the time, if that. But it was wonderful for Greg to be with a young man who taught the same types of things they were learning at home and at church. Grandpas are great, but not quite the same as a young man.

One day while Greg was at karate camp, I went to my parent's house to visit my aunt and uncle who were visiting from out of town. The place where they lived was three time zones away, so I didn't get to see them often. I had taken Kyle for a walk to the park, and he fell off a suspension bridge which was only a foot off the ground. He wasn't himself at all, so I took him to the hospital. It wasn't the same hospital that Eric had been in, but it was the emergency room. It had been four months since Eric died, so being in an emergency room was a bit traumatic for me that day. After some X-rays, it was determined that Kyle had broken his collarbone. They can't cast that of course, so he wore a sling. He called it his "strap" and felt less pain when wearing it. At least he was a less mobile unit than Greg. It would have been awful to try and keep Greg still enough to heal a broken collar bone. I think we stayed at my parent's house overnight that night in case something happened and I needed to take Kyle back to the hospital. He was OK ... as OK as one can be with a broken collar bone.

Karate camp week finished, and I was at home by myself with the boys. I was not sleeping through the night, as I had a newborn and a two-year-old with a broken bone who also needed tending to in the night. By now the baby was starting to be fussy in the evenings, which made it really difficult to get everyone else to bed. I had no idea how I would ever survive. I was so exhausted, broken hearted, discouraged, and hopeless. I didn't cry in front of the boys, but sometimes I just went into my room and laid on the floor, cried and begged God for help. When I couldn't cry anymore, I'd go back to doing what needed to be done.

I was a giant mess. My mother was coming one day a week to help, which was OK, until the day she started to cry and said she couldn't manage, so I sent her home. Another friend from my Bible study group called to see how I was doing. She asked what the most difficult things were and I told her the hardest part was the evening ... trying to do dishes and get the older boys to bed while the baby cried the whole time. *The whole time.* My friend, who didn't even go to my church, offered to create a help calendar of sorts.

Somehow she got phone numbers of people from my church, and soon I had someone coming from the church every night between 7 and 9 pm to bounce the baby, or do dishes, or fold laundry, or whatever. She gave me a copy of the schedule so I knew who was coming. That was a life saver. Those precious people from the church took time out of their busy lives to be with me in my giant mess. And my precious friend offered to do all that calling when she didn't even know the people. God was making a way. It was still extremely difficult, but extremely difficult is better than impossible.

That fall, Greg started senior kindergarten at his new school. He took the school bus, so I didn't have to take him to school, which was a welcome relief. I missed him terribly when he was at school, but having only two kids to take care of was also a relief. It seemed everything that happened was a mixed bag as far as emotions were concerned.

People from church continued to come every evening and help. One retired gentleman offered to take care of cutting the grass, which was also wonderful as our new house on the highway had a couple of acres of grass to cut.

The last day of school before Christmas, Greg came home with a fever. He had chicken pox. The other boys caught it next. The baby had a giant chicken pox blister on the roof of his mouth. He wasn't able to drink his bottle and just howled non-stop. There was a doctor who went to the church, and I phoned him. He suggested I put some freezing gel used for teething on the baby's mouth so he could drink his bottle. He was kind enough to bring some to my house. I couldn't leave without taking everyone with me, and I had already put the other boys to bed. The gel worked like a charm and the baby was able to drink his bottle. Of course it was Christmas time, probably closer to the New Year then, and it was cold and dark outside. The house had a very large country kitchen, so I put the baby in the stroller and walked him around the kitchen table until he fell asleep.

And so began the first winter in our new house. It had been an extremely gruelling ten months and I think Earl and Joan thought I should have a break. In February, Earl and Joan suggested I take Greg to Capital City for the weekend to visit Eric's friend James, who played the bagpipes at Eric's funeral. They offered to take care of Kyle and Evan while Greg and I went visiting. They probably thought I could have some kind of a break as I would only have one kid to deal with, the most capable of the three, and they could help out and only need to take care of the rest. Besides, James had a daughter about Greg's age, so he would have someone to hang out with too.

Kyle and the baby stayed with Eric's parents, while Greg and I took the train to Capital City. It was a five-hour drive and there was no way I could drive for five hours with him in the car and be able to function when we got there. Besides, Greg *loved* trains. The person at the ticket booth gave him a cardboard train to play with and he went up and down the aisle in the passenger car chatting with the other passengers.

A river ran through Capital City. It froze in the winter, and every year there was a winter festival for about ten days in February. There were snow and ice sculpture contests, and skating on the river. All along the river there were vendors with shacks set up selling hot chocolate, hot dogs, and the like. We had a wonderful time in Capital City with our friends on the first weekend of the winter festival. We even rode on what Greg called a "squeezy bus." The bus looked like two buses hooked together with an accordion. We sat in the squeezy part and Greg was thrilled. It was nice to do something different and fun.

My parents picked us up when we arrived back at the train station. My mom stayed overnight but my dad went home. The next day, my mother said she had been vomiting all night. So had the rest of North America, apparently. The Norwalk virus was in full swing everywhere. I packed up all the kids and drove my mother for 30 minutes to her house, then drove back home. I think the longest we went without someone being sick that winter was a week. Miraculously, I never got sick.

Spring eventually came and everyone was finally healthy. The baby, Evan, was a year old. We had survived that first year. Samantha, who was married to my cousin that had been killed, had become a great friend. She lived near Eric's parents, about a half hour away, so mostly we just talked on the phone. She had been going to a "widow's group." A dear lady, about an hour away, was inviting widows she knew and inviting those widows to invite widows *they* knew to a potluck at her house one Sunday per month. It was a warm, welcoming place where everyone was a widow, and everyone could share their experiences, challenges, and victories in a safe environment. There were older kids there so my boys had other kids to watch out for them. By then Greg was six, Kyle was three and a half and Evan was about a year old.

Those Sundays went by so quickly. By the time we got there and I got everyone's food sorted out, then helped the baby with his as he was only a year old, it was pretty much time to pack up and go home because it was an hour's drive. I put the guys into their pajamas because they would fall asleep in the car, and then I just carried them into the house and put them in bed. That group was a wonderful lifeline for me. People understood my predicament. You could say *anything* about anything without receiving judgement, or pat answers on what I should do. Most of the ladies were older and their kids were adults. I was 34. But still, everyone was at different stages in their widowhood, and it was encouraging to see what people were doing to cope, and feel that life would get easier someday, however hard that was to believe.

I was, and always will be, deeply and profoundly grateful to the people who helped me during that first year. That year was unimaginably difficult and I don't know what I would have done without them. Some of the people from church who helped me didn't even know me that well, but they stepped up anyway. I learned a lot about giving, receiving, my undeniable need for large amounts of help, and how incredibly kind and wonderful people could be.

Growing up, I had felt like an inconvenience to my own mother, and decided I wouldn't ask for help anymore. And I didn't ask for help, but people could see I needed it and they just came and helped me. It was very humbling. As the Bible says in Psalm 23:4, "Even though I walk through the valley of the shadow of death, I will fear no evil for you are with me (NIV)". God was with me in the form of all the wonderful people who helped me.

That situation gave me a heart of empathy for women in developing nations. From what I understand, they need help. And maybe there really isn't anyone they *can* ask for help. I still had to take care of myself and my kids, but I had help. I also had resources and opportunities, like a car for getting groceries and the ability to take a train for a weekend vacation with my six year old son. I had the life insurance payout, so I could feed my family and keep a roof over our head until I could find some work. I could take courses to become qualified to get work.

I can't go and help these women overseas, but I can send bicycles, which *will* help them get to work and feed their family. They can become bicycle mechanics and start a business servicing the bicycles in their community, and provide for their family. They can finish school and do something they would love to do. A bicycle *is* a help, a resource, and an opportunity.

A NEW BEGINNING

"They saw that the fire had not harmed their bodies, nor was a hair on their heads singed; their robes were not scorched and there was no smell of fire on them" (Daniel 3:27b NIV).

I had been contemplating what to do with the land we had—almost 13 acres. Roughly ten acres was bush. There was about a quarter acre of flat land close to the house. The rest was hilly. I thought it might be fun to grow pumpkins and have a roadside pumpkin stand. My friend who stayed with the boys the night Eric died was a farmer, so she knew about those types of things and encouraged me. I told my parents about my idea and my father flatly told me that I couldn't do that. I decided I could, and I did it.

Years later, I learned that my father had phoned my farmer friend who encouraged me to give the pumpkins a try. He reprimanded her for encouraging me to plant the pumpkins. It was bad enough that my parents didn't help or encourage certain aspects of my life, and even worse that they actively discouraged any kind of growth I was venturing upon. But to learn that my friend was called and reprimanded for her part in encouraging me actually left me feeling angry with my father, and embarrassed that my friend had to go through that. It was just pumpkins! What harm could that be?

Historically, speaking to my parents about things like that just caused more problems than it solved, so I didn't talk to my dad about it. He wasn't likely to grab me by the shoulders and start banging me against the wall, but the emotional equivalent was a possibility. I did, however, apologize to my friend for that experience. I also continued to wonder, more often and more deeply, why my family was the way they were, and why was I so different.

In any case, Earl was very gracious and brought his backhoe to pull out a few tree stumps so we would have an area to "farm." I purchased a bag of pumpkin seeds, and my lawn mowing friend brought his rototiller and tilled up some rows. We planted the seeds according to the instructions on the package, and soon enough there were many rows of little 'whale tail' plants growing. Kyle was delighted. He said, "there's a pumpkin. And there's another one, and another one, and another one!" It was fun to see the plants grow. Something was actually *fun*!

That summer, my father finished the ceiling project that Eric had started at the cottage. He took down the existing drywall ceiling and finished the bottoms of the beams. It was magnificent. He also built a third bedroom at the cottage, which was something that had been discussed over the years. Dad was semi-retired, and he spent most of the summer at the cottage building away. Late in the summer I went there with the boys for the first time in two years.

The first year after Eric died was very difficult. There was a seemingly endless string of "firsts." First Christmas without him, first birthday without him, first wedding anniversary without him. First after first after first. I just never knew when something would blindside me and leave me an emotional wreck. It seemed I wasn't done with firsts, even though two years had passed. At least I had lots of firsts under my belt and knew that it would be hard to be at the cottage without Eric. I also knew that I would be okay after a few days of sadness.

Mom and dad stayed in the new bedroom, I stayed in the middle bedroom with the baby, and the other boys stayed in the front bedroom. Mom and dad installed some bunk beds, so the following year all three boys were able to stay in the same room. The boys loved the cottage and the bunk beds.

It was hard to be there without Eric, but it was wonderful to see the beautiful work he had done on the ceiling. More mixed blessings. I was very grateful to be able to go there, see the lake and enjoy the sunshine. I was grateful that my parents were willing to have us there. The tradition became that we would go for the long weekends in the summer. That worked out to three long weekends, which was about all my parents could handle with the busyness of having three little boys around. I loved the cottage so very much and was grateful for any time I could spend there at all.

Later in September, the pumpkins were ready. My lawn mowing friend created a beautiful sign that said "PUMPKINS." It was huge! It looked like he had an old door lying around and painted it into a pumpkin sign. There were a few picnic tables and a bolt of orange fabric left behind by the previous owner of the house. We covered the picnic tables with the orange fabric. My lawn mowing friend also built a money box, which he screwed to one of the picnic tables, and gave us the key to the padlock. Earl gave me a yard trailer to use with the lawn tractor, and I piled all the guys into the yard trailer and drove out to the pumpkin patch to harvest pumpkins and put them at our roadside stand.

Kyle had started junior kindergarten, so when the boys got off the school bus they would take turns retrieving our sales from the money box and seeing how many pumpkins had sold. We took another trip out to the pumpkin patch to harvest more pumpkins and replenish our stock for sale. It was wonderful to see growth and life, even if it was just pumpkins.

That fall, as the baby approached 18 months of age, I asked God what was going to become of me. Should I look for a job? A few days later, a couple from church who owned a business phoned and asked if I would be interested in working for them a day or two a week, doing filing and odd jobs. I decided that since I had just inquired of God about that, I should take them up on their offer. My mother and father agreed to come once a week to stay with whoever was home at the time. Around here, kindergarten (junior and senior) was all day, every other day. We did Mondays, Wednesdays, and every other Friday. Another day each week Sheryl, the pastor's wife, would come and stay with whoever was here. And so I re-entered the workforce doing filing, my 98th percentile skill.

As time went on with this little job, I learned that my friends had a contract bookkeeper. They asked her to show me how to enter invoices on the computer, so I could do that instead of her. This gave me more things to do, and kept their costs down. Over time, I remembered that I was going to do the bookkeeping for Eric's business. This lady did bookkeeping for lots of people's businesses. I could do that!

I took some bookkeeping courses and I also did a course in the accounting software that was being used. It was really helpful to actually be working in the software at the same time I was doing the course. The course was at a local community college, and it was a night course, so I needed people to stay with the boys while I did that. I think Earl and Joan did so. I loved the idea of being a contract bookkeeper as that would give me control over when and how much work I had. I could work from home, and as the boys became more self-sufficient, I could take on more work. I didn't want to work full time, because the boys had already lost their dad, and I didn't want to be gone from them all the time either. During school, it was fine, but what about the summer, Christmas, and spring break? Besides, Greg was in martial arts and his classes were around 5:00 pm. This way I was available to take him to his classes. Kyle had also started martial arts. Joe, our instructor, was *amazing* with the boys. They learned focus, self-discipline, self-control, and had the chance to run around and yell, which is something they couldn't do at school.

As time went on, I took over more and more of the work from the contract bookkeeper at my friend's business. Eventually she moved away, and I was officially the bookkeeper. By then, the baby was three and I had him in daycare two days per week like I had done with the other boys. Two days a week helped us all to ease into them being gone when the time came for them to go to school. The other boys were in school full time, so the days when Evan was in daycare, I worked. Greg was eight and Kyle was five. Kyle had a November birthday, so he started school when he was still three. He could barely haul himself up the steps of the bus with his backpack on, and I was sure I had lost my mind sending an almost-four-year-old to school on the bus. But his big brother went to school on the bus, so he wanted to go as well.

The Pixar Movie *Finding Nemo* came out in 2003. We didn't go to the theatre for anything, but we did rent videos from the video store in town. I remember watching the movie and feeling like Marlin, the father clownfish. Coral, the mother clownfish had died trying to save all of their eggs, and only Nemo, with his gimpy fin, had survived. Poor Marlin was quite neurotic and overprotective of Nemo.

I did not want to be neurotic and overprotective of my sons, but I was. Nemo and Marlin went through some hard things, but in the end, everything turned out well for Nemo. He was fine, and his relationship with his dad was fine. Better, actually. Perhaps taking life lessons from an animated children's film might not be the best idea, but the learning curve on reinventing myself and raising three boys by myself was intensely steep. The whole film really resonated with me. Things were really hard at the beginning for Nemo and his dad, but they hung in there, had some help from various sources, and everything turned out alright in the end. That was what I wanted for my sons and myself, to overcome any challenge that came our way and have it be all right in the end.

Thanks to Nemo, I remembered the fiery furnace in Daniel, where the three men went in and didn't even smell like smoke when they came out. I had decided that was going to be me. Nemo and Marlin showed me that I would need to do things a different way if that was going to be true for me and my family. I doubled down on my resolve, and decided that not only was I going to survive Eric dying, but I was going to thrive. I was going to thrive not in spite of it, but because of it. The Lord really does work in mysterious ways.

THERE ARE NO OBSTACLES, ONLY OPPORTUNITIES.

"The Lord turned to him and said, 'Go in the strength you have. Am I not sending you?'" (Judges 6:14 NIV).

My sons were a busy bunch, and they all loved Lego. There was a Lego store about an hour from our house that had a great selection, as well as a racing ramp and tables of Lego set up all over the place. A person could build a car with the available Lego, and then send it down the five-lane ramp, which had a handle that released all five lanes at the same time. Taking the boys there on spring break became an annual event. In the early years, we would be at the store for a couple of hours, and when everyone started to get hungry, we would go for pizza afterward. Evan was probably less than a year old the first year we went there, and he was in the stroller the whole time.

As the boys got older and I could leave them in the store by themselves for a few minutes, I would bring snacks so they could go out to the car as needed to have their snack. This allowed us to stay at the store building cars for up to five or six hours. They loved building cars and racing them, and we always went out for pizza afterward. I was no good with Lego, but I could look for pieces for them. So my job was to look for a certain piece in a certain colour. As the boys became teenagers, they were these huge dudes sitting at these tiny chairs building their cars and having a fun time, and the little kids would just sit and watch them build. We always bought some Lego at the store, and it was a much-anticipated annual event. We still went even when Greg was 18 and had a full beard.

In the spring of 2006, Evan turned four. I was *the* bookkeeper at my friend's business, and was becoming more comfortable and efficient at doing the work. I was working two full days per week, and taking Greg and Kyle to martial arts classes what seemed like every evening. They were doing great in school, we looked forward to spending time at the cottage during the summer, and the monthly widow's group meetings were wonderful for all of us.

Joe, our martial arts instructor, was offering a self defence class for women. I decided to take it, and it was so great I decided to sign up for ongoing martial arts training. I couldn't ride my bike because I couldn't leave the house without a lot of fanfare. Joe said it would be okay with him if I left the boys to fend for themselves in the dressing room on Saturdays so I could take the adult class. I arranged for a babysitter one night per week so I could do another class. Two classes a week wasn't enough to become proficient, but twice a week was better than nothing. A lovely university student from church said she would babysit. She had her own car, which was also necessary as I couldn't drive her home either. My house on the highway was a place one had to drive to, or take a cab, as it was too far out of town to walk, and there was no public transit.

I was scared out of my mind at my first class in my white uniform with my white belt. I think there was one other adult woman in the class. The rest were men and teenage boys, with few teenage girls. Although I was afraid, I pressed on because it looked fun, and I remembered missing out on going to Calgary when I was 12 because I was afraid. I didn't want fear to have a deciding voice in any decision I made ever again. Even though I had been doing an exercise plan of sorts, it was *nothing* compared to martial arts. I was sore every day for months. And then I tested for my yellow belt, which made me even more sore. I began to realize that there was a direct connection between my emotional self and my physical self. If I was having a super difficult day, it was easier to be patient and just calmly do what needed to be done because I knew I had martial arts that night. And in class there was so much physical activity that stress and frustration just seemed to melt away. I was in love with martial arts.

The boys were very well behaved on Saturdays when I had my class, which was after their class. We agreed that if they were well behaved, we could get some treats at Tim Horton's on the way home. I did bring things for them to do, and the class was only an hour, so it worked out really well.

I liked to have "special time" with each boy so I could give them my undivided attention. When Kyle was in grade four, around eight or nine years old, I took him to the Science Centre. We took the train, the subway, and the bus. We spent more time travelling than we did at the Science Centre, but we were able to see a documentary about insects in the rainforest in the Imax Theatre. Kyle loved bugs, so that was a great movie. We lived in a rural area, so the train, subway, and bus were a great experience for him also. Another time I drove him to the Bird Aviary. They had a reptile section and

I have a photo of him with Phoenix the python around his shoulders. Phoenix was a small python, only six feet long. I have a photo of Kyle holding three bearded dragons as well. I had never seen a happier kid. It was wonderful to be with Kyle, seeing what he wanted to see and moving at his pace. He also loved puppets, and the gift shop had a beautiful macaw puppet. Kyle rarely asked for anything, so when he asked for the macaw puppet, I had to get it for him.

Greg and I would go out for breakfast on a regular basis for our special time, but Kyle seemed to prefer bigger events less often, like the bird aviary, to more regular restaurant visits. Evan preferred regular restaurant visits too, but he liked to go to Subway for a ham sandwich. I think that was a kids' meal of some kind, and he didn't want anything on his sandwich but ketchup, which wasn't even an option at Subway! They found some packages of ketchup for him and he was happy. I didn't understand why he liked to go to Subway and not get any of the sandwich toppings, but that was what he liked. The first time we went to Subway, just Evan and me, he put on his dress shirt and clip-on tie that had transport trucks on it. He was about five years old then, and the sweetest little boy ever. Greg progressed well through his martial arts training—he was a natural. On his tenth birthday, Greg tested for his black belt. Joe's position was that the kids would do all the same things the adults did, so it was a full black belt. Greg had to do a "bootcamp" to get ready for the test, and he had to keep a journal of what he ate. One bit of junk food a week was all that was allowed. Joe believed that a person was not a black belt if they couldn't control what went in their mouth. All the black belt candidates also had to intentionally perform random acts of kindness, and write them in their journal. Journals were spot checked. If you didn't bring it and you were asked for it, you were dismissed and not allowed to test. If you brought the journal but were not keeping up with what was expected, you were dismissed and not allowed to test. I loved these character-building high expectations.

Greg was very fond of Joe. In fact, Greg had been helping teach some classes to the really young kids. Toward the end of Greg's four-hour black belt test, there was an especially gruelling requirement. The last part was the only part of the test where spectators were allowed. Greg was doing awesome, and I yelled as much, cheering him on with everything I had, something I had never heard from my parents. Joe told me after the test that he was really impressed with Greg, that he had finished strong. On the way home, I picked up a pizza for Greg since he hadn't had one in a while, and asked him if he could hear me cheering. He said he could, and that he couldn't have done it without me. Greg and I had always had a special relationship. Maybe it was because we were both first born, or because he is like his dad. That day was very special for me, seeing him perform like that, five years after his father died. Yes, we were going to be okay.

He was in grade five the year he turned ten, and his teacher did *not* like him. I don't know what happened, but my belief is that because she had a degree in psychology, she decided he was a problem because he came from a single parent home. Until then, he had not been a problem. That school year was a complete nightmare for him. Between snow days and mental health days, he missed a lot of school. It was really hard to send him to school when most days he would start to cry as soon as he got off the bus. Meetings with the teacher and principal (who were both women) only made things worse. The vice principal was a man, and he invited Greg to be on the wrestling team. He was so lovely to Greg and to me. I really felt like he disagreed with what was happening with Greg but could do little about it. Greg did well on the wrestling team. He won some of the matches at the tournament, and had his name in the local paper.

The school situation became almost unbearable. I was at the school a lot, like many other parents, to speak to the principal about this teacher. At the end of the school year, I learned that the teacher had been transferred to another school to teach kindergarten for the following year, which meant we wouldn't need to deal with her ever again.

My friend Crystal had two kids the same ages as Kyle and Evan. Her marriage ended a few months after her second baby was born, the same year that Eric died. We knew each other from church, although not very well. She had offered to take care of Kyle during Eric's funeral, and we spent a lot of time together after her marriage ended. Sundays were hard for us as the dads were absent. We took turns having Sunday supper at each other's house. We had another adult to speak with, and the kids played together, so it was nice for everyone.

A friend recommended a TV show called *Enjoying Everyday Life* with Joyce Meyer, which was just snippets of Joyce's conference teachings. I enjoyed the show and watched it every day. Those teachings were life changing for me. Joyce had an amazing way of explaining scripture and applying it to things we deal with on a daily basis. As Crystal and I spent more time together, I learned that she watched Joyce Meyer's program as well!

Crystal and I went to the Joyce Meyer Women's Convention in St. Louis a couple of times. We drove to Detroit, which was about three hours from our homes, and flew to St. Louis. It was a wonderful adventure and deeply moving experience to be with 25,000 other women hearing Joyce's teaching, along with other speakers.

I learned a lot from Joyce Meyer. She was open about sharing that she was sexually abused by her father until she left home at age 18. That would not be an easy way to live, but there she was speaking to thousands of people at conferences every weekend, had a TV show, and books she had written available for sale in two thirds of the world. Joyce's teaching gave me a great deal of hope. I would share what I was learning from watching Joyce's show with Crystal. On some level, I knew that I was making myself vulnerable to Crystal. I wanted her to feel emotionally safe with me. I wanted to be close friends with her. But no matter how vulnerable I left myself, she held me at arm's length. Since I hadn't yet learned about emotional boundaries, I continued to make myself emotionally vulnerable, even though that was not being fully reciprocated.

One summer Crystal and I went to Six Flags Darien Lake for the Christian music festival called Kingdom Bound. There were some artists there we wanted to see, but we also did some roller coasters and had a fun day. I have a picture of us from the roller coaster camera. It was a really fun day.

Several years prior to that, I had gone to Darien Lake for the Kingdom Bound festival by myself. Jeremy Camp was performing there, and he was also doing a meet and greet. I couldn't get anyone to go with me, so I went alone. I wanted to see Jeremy's concert and meet him. He had written a song called "I Still Believe" which was deeply moving for me. As a young man, he had gotten married, and his wife died of cancer within a year or so afterwards. The song was about God's faithfulness and trusting Him even though things are intensely painful and don't make any sense. Jeremy became a very successful worship singer, and a movie was even made about his experience. Anyway, I wanted to meet him, and I did. It was really awesome.

I was still part of the "Hands in Praise" ladies group that signed to songs, and we began having the meetings at my house so I wouldn't have to get a babysitter. I taught myself the signs to Jeremy's "I Still Believe" song, and signed by myself for the church one Sunday. That turned out to be the Sunday all the boys had chicken pox, so I needed a team of grandparents to deal with them so I could get to the church.

About four years after Eric died, I began to wonder what it would be like to be in a relationship with a man other than Eric. Around that time, a local church was having a singles event, so I went. Crystal wasn't interested, so I went alone. I was learning that if I wanted to do anything, I might have to do it alone, or not at all. Anyway, I attended the event and met a lovely man there. He lived out of town, so I only saw him a couple of times per month. I knew that relationships took time, and a few hours per month was not a lot of time. The university student who babysat when I went to martial arts during the week was able to stay with the boys when I went out with Frank.

In time, Crystal met a lovely man and they decided to get married. She asked me to be her matron of honour. I accepted. I was happy for Crystal, but she was moving on with her life, and things were still the same for me, so I did wonder what I would do with myself. I knew that God's plan for Crystal was different from His plan for me. What He was doing for her He would also do for me, in His perfect timing.

I was involved in some of Crystal's wedding planning activities, so the concept of "as long as we both shall live" was on my mind. I decided that I couldn't see myself being married to Frank, even though he was very nice. I had been seeing him for several months but the relationship seemed to have plateaued. It wasn't bad, but it wasn't awesome either, and didn't seem like it would be awesome any time soon, so I ended our relationship the week before Crystal's wedding. That was hard to do, but I knew in my heart he wasn't the right man for me. I thought the sooner we parted ways the sooner we could both move on. I also wanted to avoid the possibility of people at Crystal's wedding asking us when we were going to get married.

I had a beautiful new dress for Crystal's wedding and had my hair and makeup done that morning. I was very happy for Crystal and her soon to be husband, but I was also sad for the relationship I had just ended, even though I was sure it was the right thing to do.

I had arranged for a babysitter for the boys, as I would be gone all day. She was having a "traditional" wedding with the white gown, church service, photos, dinner and speeches. During the speeches, Crystal talked about what a great friend I was and about all the fun things we had done together, none of which she had done before. But then she said that I had offered her the book *How to Get a Date Worth Keeping,* and she refused because she was expecting to just find someone to marry without going into any of the dating business. Her speech concluded with, "And now I'm married."

I felt completely humiliated. I was attending the wedding alone, and at that moment wished the earth would open up and swallow me whole. I'm not sure what her intention was with that speech, but what I heard was, "My friend is really great, we have done lots of things together that I have never done before, and we have had lots of fun. But as fun and great as my friend is, now I'm married and she isn't." At that moment, I was sorry I had shared my heart with her. Suddenly our whole friendship seemed like a competition she had won, I had lost, and she made a point of sharing that with everyone at her wedding reception.

In the weeks that followed, she expressed concern about spending time with me because she was married and I wasn't. I reminded her that I spent time with married people every day at work or martial arts, so that was a nonissue. God's plan for me was different than it was for her. That being said, I wasn't sure where she was coming from. I felt betrayed and humiliated and was quite happy that she would be spending all her time with her husband instead of with me. Friends don't generally leave their friends feeling betrayed and humiliated in a public setting. I don't like competition. "A rising tide lifts all boats" is more what I'm about. Iron sharpening iron. Let's work together and help each other grow, learn and become. My attempts to help Crystal feel emotionally safe with me were unsuccessful. I wondered if she had been competing with me the whole time and I just didn't know it. Perhaps that's why she was reluctant to share what she was learning and how she was feeling. Until she shared, publicly, that she had won, and I had lost.

As expected, Crystal was busy with her new husband and her new life, so we didn't spend much time together after that. This was fine with me, as dealing with difficult situations like I perceived I was in after her wedding speech was something I was *not* good at. Having the situation resolve itself organically was the preferred option for me. I would see her at church, say hello to her and her husband and be pleasant, but that was about it. She sat with her husband in church, and I sat by myself.

At martial arts, Joe started teaching a leadership program on Saturdays and invited Greg to participate. It was amazing. Greg went to his own classes and helped teach in Kyle's class. Evan was five then and started taking martial arts as well. We were there anyway, and it was awesome. Classes went by belts, not by age, so lots of times Kyle and Evan were in the same class, which Greg helped to teach. When they got home from school they would have a quick snack and go to martial arts, then come home for supper. Some nights I had a class as well, so back to the dojo I would go, once the babysitter arrived. Joe invited me to be in the leadership program as well. He had read a lot on personal development, which I also did, and much of what he said in the leadership class really resonated with me. I loved that my son was hearing about things at the age of ten that I was just learning in my late 30's. I always thought it funny that my worst subjects in school were math and phys-ed, and here I was working as a bookkeeper and taking martial arts.

I loved martial arts because Joe, who competed internationally and won, would show us something that he was going to teach us, and I would think there was no way I could do that. But he would break the move down into small parts, and with our partner we would practice the small parts, and then put the whole thing together. Of course, my attempts were nowhere near what Joe could do, but I still made them. That was a major life lesson for me. Even if things seemed daunting and impossible, if I could just break it down into small parts and work on those, everything would come together in time, as long as I was persistent, diligent, and determined, which I was.

The year Greg turned 12, Sophie, the secretary/treasurer at the church, was having knee replacement surgery. She worked half days, every day. My boss also went to the church and suggested I could take over until Sophie was able to resume work. Everyone liked that idea, and by then Evan was in school full time, so that worked out. I worked mornings at one job and afternoons at the other. That project lasted about nine months. In the summer, I could work while Greg stayed with the other boys. With the church job being over in the summer, I only had my other job. I still went only in the mornings, with Greg holding down the fort while I worked. In the afternoons I had them in swimming lessons, and we would go to the park and do other things that were fun.

In time, I had made my way through the belts and was ready to test for my own black belt. When I started martial arts training, I had thought of it as just fun fitness. Somewhere along the line, I began to believe I could actually become a black belt. The martial arts school we attended also had a fitness program, and it was tough. I loved it. Greg would partner with me in the fitness classes and it was awesome to work with my son in that way. I brought things for the other boys to do and they were very good at entertaining themselves in the waiting area while Greg and I did our fitness class. Here I was, six months past my 40th birthday, testing for a black belt. I practiced the things I needed to practice at home. I did my running, fitness classes, and regular classes. I was fully invested in succeeding with my black belt test.

The day of the test was a Saturday. I remember being scared out of my mind and wondering why I thought I could do this. Then a thought came to me: "Remember Gideon." I looked up the story of Gideon in Judges chapter six. In his own estimation, Gideon was the weakest man in the weakest clan, yet God approached him and addressed him as a "mighty warrior." Gideon complained and was fearful, but God said, "Go in the strength you have. Am I not sending you?" Although I was still frightened, I felt like everything would turn out fine if I would go in the strength I had. I had worked very hard for a long time, so I was prepared. And I did *not* want to let fear have a deciding vote like it did when I missed my chance to go to Calgary. So I packed up my gear and my snacks and went to the dojo.

Evan had a birthday party to go to that day, so my parents came to take him to and from the birthday party. The last hour of the four-hour black belt test allowed spectators, so mother and pa were going to bring the boys to the test as well. The last hour of the test arrived, and so did the spectators. I had felt my strength fading at one point during the test, but strength came from somewhere and I was able to continue. The last part of the test was particularly gruelling because there were spectators. Or maybe it just felt more gruelling because we had been doing gruelling things for a few hours by that point.

After we did all that was required, the time to hand out the black belts had arrived. Joe gave all of us black belt candidates a rose. He told us that we all had people supporting us through our black belt journey, and we were to give the rose to the person who had been most supportive. I went straight to Greg and gave him the rose. He had given up his class time and watched his brothers so I could do extra classes in preparation for my test. I could not have done it without him, and I told him that when I gave him the rose. That is exactly what he said to me two years earlier when he tested for his black belt and I asked him if he could hear me cheering. My son and I empowered each other to do something amazing, and that experience drew us very close together. We always had a very special relationship, but helping each other to become black belts cemented that relationship in ways that words cannot express.

After I took off my red belt and tied my hard-won black belt around my 40-year-old waist, I picked up a pizza, just like after Greg's test. Joe was the first person since Eric to actively believe in me. Or at least that is how it felt. He told me that I was 1 percent of 1 percent. It was because of Joe that I had signed up for martial arts. It was because of Joe and his teaching and his constant way of adding value to my precious sons and to me that I was able to complete my black belt journey. I will be forever grateful to him for the difference he made in our lives.

My parents came back to the house with us for our pizza party. Mother was very snarly. She didn't speak to me or look at me, and she looked super angry. I couldn't understand that—becoming a black belt was a significant accomplishment for me. Not only was she not happy for me, she was angry.

Around the time I felt betrayed and humiliated at Crystal's wedding, things came to a head with Jack, the man who had been cutting my grass. The boys were getting older and I had taught Greg how to drive the lawn tractor. I could also cut the grass myself because I could leave the boys in the house, unlike when they were babies/toddlers. They were old enough to come out and get me if necessary, and they were responsible enough to manage while I was outside for a couple of hours.

Jack started to invent reasons to come to my house. He had projects he wanted to do here, since he wasn't really needed for cutting grass anymore. He would show up uninvited and unannounced, stating that we would be moving firewood that day, or whatever. I didn't like that, especially when he would show up around the time the boys caught the bus to school and I was still in my pajamas. He had also gotten into the habit of coming into the house for a coffee after he had finished mowing, which seemed fine for a while. He was like another dad to me. Serving him a coffee seemed like the least I could do since he had driven from his house and spent two hours mowing my grass.

The problem was that he started talking about things that made me uncomfortable. Sexual things. I told him I was uncomfortable talking about that and his answer was, "Why are you uncomfortable? People do it, why can't we talk about it?"

Well, he was old enough to be my father, and I didn't feel that was an appropriate conversation, regardless of his age. I was feeling increasingly uncomfortable with him. I began to consider selling my house and moving into town. That idea felt really awful, and I searched myself for why I was pursuing that idea. I realized I thought that if I had a smaller house and property in town, it would be easy to tell Jack we could manage fine and not have him come around anymore. It was then that God said to me, "What are you doing? I gave you this house and I will give you the resources to take care of it." So ended my quest to look for houses in town. I breathed a sigh of relief and at once felt at peace with my decision to remain in the home I loved.

As difficult as it was, I also decided to tell Jack that we could take care of the grass ourselves. The boys were old enough to help, so it was time for us to fly solo. I thanked him for all he had done over the years and told him that we wouldn't be where we were without his help. He lost it. Yelled at me. Went on about my ungratefulness and temerity to do such a thing after all he had done for me. All this, even though I thanked him profusely for all his help. When the "helper calendar" had no longer been needed several years prior, I thanked all the people who had helped me and gave them gifts. They were happy to have helped, and happy I was in a place to be able to manage myself. I had expected the same from Jack. His reaction just confirmed to me that something had gone sideways with the lawn mowing arrangement.

In the weeks that followed, he phoned me several times per day. I knew it was him because I had a caller ID. I didn't answer the phone. He also drove by my house a lot. That was something I hadn't noticed before, and I noticed everything, so I figured that was new behaviour. It was all very creepy. I took to locking the door during the day, just in case. He and his wife stopped coming to church, which was fine by me.

Situations like that made it hard not to feel sorry for myself. Being widowed is "the gift that keeps on giving," one of my widowed friends would often say. The monthly potluck at her house was really nice for that reason. We were all in various places along the being widowed timeline, and to hear other people's experience was helpful. At least things like the grass cutting man going sideways didn't feel personal. Some of the other widows had dealt with men in a variety of capacities, usually in a helping situation, where the helping arrangement had stopped due to sexually inappropriate behaviour by the men. I was sorry some of the widows had experienced that, as it was incredibly difficult and unpleasant. However, I was very grateful for a safe environment to share about the situation I experienced. I was even more grateful to have people truly understand what that was like. They assured me that what happened with Jack was *not my fault*.

And there was hope. We were all getting on with our lives in our various ways, and sharing our struggles and successes was wonderful.

Like the time Greg needed to wear a tie for something. I had no idea how to tie a tie. Eric knew, but he was gone. So I googled that and found a YouTube video on how to tie a tie. We used one of Eric's ties. I managed to tie the tie, and told Greg to just pull it over his head and tighten/loosen as needed so we didn't have to figure out how to tie it again. There were so many small things like that, to remind us that there was a hole in our family. But the flip side was that we managed anyway.

I also used YouTube to figure out how to change the faucet in the shower and the element in my oven. Yes, if Eric were here he could have done that, but I was able to empower myself to do it. I realized I was really very capable and resourceful. Bittersweet. That kind of summed up life at that time. Things were often very challenging, but I was managing. I believe it was Eleanor Roosevelt who said, "Women are like teabags … you don't know how strong you are until you are in hot water." I loved that. I also loved the motivational sign that said, "The voice in your head that says you can't do this is a liar." I had that as the background on my computer for a long time, to remind myself that I was a victor, not a victim.

In addition to the semi-regular "special time" I had with each son, I wanted to do something extra special when they turned 13. Greg really liked music, so we did a couple of fun things. There was a show at a nearby venue with an orchestra that was playing Star Wars music. Greg was a hard-core Star Wars fan, and I wanted him to have some kind of culture, so I bought tickets to the show. Anthony Daniels, the voice of

C3PO, was the host of the show. He basically told the Star Wars story. Between his narratives, the orchestra played the music and clips from the movie were played on the big screen to show what Anthony Daniels had been explaining. It was really something to see a live orchestra. There were people there in costume and it was a really fun event. Being able to enjoy the evening with Greg at his pace and not have to keep track of his brothers was wonderful. I also took him to see a Def Leppard concert. A proper rock concert for the 13-year-old. We had floor seats and it was an amazing show. He was in awe at both events. It was like when he was a toddler and saw snow for the first time.

I am a human woman, and my strength is limited. God's strength is endless, and is deeply powerful. In Judges 6:14 God says, "Go in the strength you have, am I not sending you?" I also love the verse in 2 Corinthians 12:8 where Paul says that God told him God's strength was made perfect in Paul's weakness. To go in the strength I had and trust that God's strength would make up the difference was a life changing concept for me. I could only do what I could do, physically and emotionally. But *God* can do anything and his strength is made perfect in my weakness. Going forth and doing the best I could with what I had allowed God to show his hand, his amazing, perfect strength. He never failed, and was always amazing.

THE RELENTLESS PURSUIT
OF CONSTANT AND
GRADUAL IMPROVEMENT

"Guard my life and rescue me; let me not be put to shame, for I take refuge in you" (Psalm 25:20 NIV).

In 2011, Greg was 14, Kyle was 12 and Evan was nine. I was still working part time at my friend's business and I was ready to take on more work. That, and there was friction between the boss and his staff. I spent a lot of time listening to the staff complain about him. I guess I was viewed as the "office manager" as well as the bookkeeper, and lots of the staff would come to me to vent, or for advice. I wanted everyone to feel encouraged and appreciated, but all of that was beginning to take its toll on me.

I decided I wanted to start my own bookkeeping business. The boys were all in school full time, so I was able to take on more work, and there wasn't more work to take on where I was working. I was also feeling mired in office politics, which would not be a thing if I had my own roster of clients.

There was a national organization called Certified Professional Bookkeepers (CPB). Bookkeeping was not a regulated industry, meaning anyone could call themselves a bookkeeper and hire themselves out as such even if they didn't have two clues about bookkeeping to rub together. Education was important to me, and I probably still felt inadequate because I only went to community college, not university. Whatever the reason, I decided to become a certified member of CPB. I would feel better about myself, that I really was qualified to do the work, and be able to communicate that to prospective clients. I was concerned I wouldn't pass the exam, so I did an online course with Universal Accounting. It was a fantastic program. I finished it with 100 percent. So I registered with CPB, purchased their handbook, and read it. I had to do the exam in a proctored setting, and my accountant agreed to let me do the test in his office.

On May 4, 2011, I passed the CPB exam with 91 percent, and became a Certified Professional Bookkeeper with a national organization. I was hired by a local bookkeeper to fill in for a maternity leave, a one year contract. The job was eight hours a week, so I did Monday and Tuesday mornings. That way, come summer, I would only be gone for two half days, which worked better for me with all the guys being home. I figured they could manage alone for two half days better than a full day. I loved the idea of working for a bookkeeping firm so I could learn the admin side of managing multiple clients. It was a great arrangement, and I learned a lot. The gentleman who hired me went on to become a CPB as well. He even referred work to me from time to time.

Around that time, the church secretary/treasurer decided she would like to retire. I had filled in for her a couple of years prior when she had knee replacement surgery, so when I offered to take over as a contract bookkeeper, the church was happy to split the secretary and treasurer duties so I could do the church books from my own office. My very first customer. Between the contract job, working at my friend's business, and the church job, I was busy. I decided to "retire" from my friend's business, because I ultimately wanted to be running my own business and not be an employee.

There was a cubby room in the basement of my house, so I bought paint and carpet and fixed it up into an office. I moved the desk in there, bought a computer and some software, and voila, bookkeeping business!

As the contract job would be coming to an end soon, I knew I had to have more than one customer. I hired a marketing consultant from Universal Accounting, with whom I did the bookkeeping training, to help me acquire more customers. It was a weekly phone call from a southern gentleman named Rick. He lived in North Carolina. I was scared out of my mind, so I found his voice and southern drawl very comforting. I did what he told me to do, and out of ten attempts, I acquired six customers.

I almost didn't hire Rick. I had scheduled a meeting with an onboarding specialist to determine if their program would be a good fit for me. The hotel we were to meet at was almost an hour from my house. That was before I had GPS or automated navigation systems. I only had a paper map. Somewhere along the line, I took a wrong turn and got lost. I was going to be late. *Very late.* I had to choose between going back home with my tail between my legs, saying that "I tried" and feeling like a loser, or pressing on and being late for the meeting, hoping for the best.

I pressed on and arrived an hour late for my meeting. I had missed the whole thing. As "luck" would have it, the person scheduled to go after me didn't show up, so I took the next time slot and had my meeting anyway. I signed the marketing consultant because I knew I needed help to make my bookkeeping business a success. Failure was not an option, and I would do whatever it took to get my new business off the ground.

I had such great success with Rick and his marketing program that Universal Accounting paid me to come and speak at their events at that hotel a couple of times per year. Their events were free, and people could come for the three-hour meeting to learn about the program. They wanted me there to share my experience and my success so that people would believe the program was real, and that they too could start a successful bookkeeping business if they hired Universal Accounting. I got to meet Rick at one of those meetings. I was so grateful to him and the help and support he had given me as I went from widowed housewife to business owner.

Public speaking was *not* my thing. I read somewhere the number one fear of most people is public speaking. That was me for sure. However, I was so grateful to Universal Accounting and everything I had accomplished through their program that I was okay with struggling through a public speaking event. My hope was that what I had to say might encourage and inspire someone else to empower themselves to succeed at their own bookkeeping business. It was easy enough to come up with what to say. I only had to explain what happened to me, so I knew the content very well.

Part of the promise of the Universal Accounting program was access to an accounting specialist who could help with questions that would come up as one went along with their new bookkeeping business. I took full advantage of that help as I started doing the books for my six new clients. I was so grateful for it.

I don't know if the boys understood what it was like for me to reinvent myself. To quit my job, start a business and go looking for customers, not knowing how that would work. That the main reason why I was doing things that way was so that I didn't have to be gone all the time at a full-time job. I wanted to be with them, available for them. To help with homework, and take them to activities like martial arts and swimming lessons. They did help me move the desk into my new cubby of an office. The desk was huge, and the people we bought the house from probably planned to use that room as a bar. Plumbing for a sink was roughed in, and there was a *large* window into the rec-room area. We decided it would be easier to get the desk into that room through the window than trying to muscle it through the doorway. So Greg, Kyle, and I did just that. It was interesting that they were getting to a point where they could help me with things like this.

That summer, Evan wanted to go to an overnight summer camp. They had a short-week option, which was Monday to Friday. He went by himself. He was great at meeting people and making friends. I despised camp, and couldn't understand for the life of me why he would want to go, but he did. I was impressed and proud of him for going alone. That struck me as very brave, especially since it was a horse camp where they rode horses and did all kinds of cool activities. It was weirdly quiet without him at home that week. Friday finally came and I went and picked him up. He had a lovely week, but didn't say much about the camp nor ask to go back the following year. He was always trying something new, just to see what it would be like.

In contrast to the success I was experiencing in launching my own bookkeeping business, that summer, our beloved cat, Hobbes, died. She was a gray tabby cat weeks away from being 20 years old. She was such a special cat. We were all devastated. Greg was only 14—she had been there his whole life. To help ease our sadness, we went to East Side Mario's for supper. We had pizza on the patio that hot August evening, and stopped at the local cruise night on the way home. A gentleman there had an orange VW van, a "hippie van" as Greg called it. Greg loved hippie vans, and the owner of the van was delighted to give us a tour.

Even though it was a sad day, we had a lovely meal together and a fun time touring the "nacho bus" as the license plate read. We even have a picture of Greg with the orange hippie van. Life is so often a mixed bag of events and emotions, but it goes on.

That fall, a friend of mine had secured a discount with Great Wolf Lodge, a hotel with an indoor water park, so I bought some tickets. We went for about three days and had an absolute blast. It was nice that the boys were getting older and we could do things like that. We did that a couple of times, and also went on a few day-trips to a water park in a neighbouring city. I was from that city and had gone to that water park when I was young. It was a water park, but they also had go karts, bumper boats, mini golf, a ropes course, rock climbing wall, and all kinds of stuff like that. We would pack a picnic lunch and snacks and just hang out there for the day doing all the activities. We didn't take big holidays as I simply didn't have the money for that. Between long weekends at the cottage and a few trips like the water parks with picnic lunches, we did have some really fun times.

In Psalm 25:2 the writer asks God to guard him and rescue him, and not let him be put to shame. I could totally understand that. What I could do was limited. I was spread very thin taking care of my home, my property, my sons, myself, and starting a business. If I needed anything at that time, I needed God to guard me and rescue me and to not let me be put to shame. I needed my little business to succeed so I could provide for my family and still be available for them. I needed protection for myself and my sons so that we would remain in good health. I needed to be rescued from whatever "you can't do that" thoughts reared their ugly heads in my mind, threatening to derail my success. God is faithful, and for that I am eternally grateful.

DECISIONS AND THE
END OF AN ERA

"Humble yourselves, therefore, under God's mighty hand, that he may lift you up in due time. Cast all your anxiety on him, because he cares for you" (1 Peter 5:6 NIV).

I don't know what happened in 2012, but it was a very tumultuous year. My business was going well, and that was a pretty steep learning curve. Good, yet I constantly felt that I didn't know what I was doing. It was really unsettling. The martial arts school moved to a neighbouring city, as Joe, our beloved instructor, sold it and moved out west with his wife. Kyle did his black belt test with Joe before he moved, so that was wonderful.

The new owners of the martial arts school were nice enough, but we didn't like the new curriculum. Greg was in high school then, and had been helping teach martial arts for the past five years. He continued to help the new owners with the teaching. He learned all things martial arts so quickly. Between the four of us, we were still at the martial arts school every day. The new owners of the school wanted everyone to test for their black belt with the new curriculum. All four of us began that process. I ended up getting injured and could not continue. Greg, Kyle, and Evan all went through the multi-stage process of black belt testing, and all achieved their black belt with the new curriculum. So Greg and Kyle had two black belts, one from Joe's school and one from the new owners, and Evan had one from the new school.

That summer, our septic tank backed up. It was a nightmare. I was concerned we would need a whole new system, which would be $30,000 I didn't have. A local septic service was able to work on the system. We couldn't really send much down the drain. Doing so made sewage bubble up all over the furnace room floor. I washed the dishes in plastic bins and dumped the water outside. Minimal flushing. The boys showered at the dojo. The ladies' changing room didn't have a shower, but a friend from martial arts lived in an apartment near us. She was going to the east coast for a two-week vacation. I volunteered to take care of her cat, and she agreed I could shower at her place, so that was nice. While the guys were at martial arts, I did laundry at the laundromat across the road from the martial arts school. That lasted most of the summer. Even when my friend returned from the east coast, I still showered at her house after she went to work. Some people are truly amazing.

Things being so difficult left me with a not very good mindset. Having a crummy mindset just led to more crummy things happening. It was a downward spiral. That year, I decided to google something. Tension was mounting between my mother and I, again. I had been doing well. I became a black belt, quit my job, and started a bookkeeping business. I was making more money in my business than I had at my job. I did *all* my work from home so I could be there for my sons and see that everyone got to their martial arts classes.

We were all happy, healthy, and fit. We were able to go to the cottage by ourselves now that the guys were old enough for me to manage.

The only time we saw my parents was on holidays, which was how I liked it. The constant digs and jabs from my mother whenever I saw her were leaving me ready to blow a gasket. We never had a good relationship. As a kid, I often felt like an inconvenience, especially when she did things like leave me at the mall. I was in my early 40's then, and she was still treating me like she had when I was a kid. I had suspected something for many years, but was barely able to think the words in my mind, much less say them out loud because it seemed so unthinkable and ridiculous.

Finally, I googled: "mothers who are jealous of their daughters." There. I did it. A tsunami of information appeared on my screen. I purchased a book called *Will I Ever Be Good Enough? Healing the Daughters of Narcissistic Mothers*, by Dr. Karyl McBride. Dr. McBride was a family therapist and had lots of field experience. Her own mother was narcissistic, so she also understood what that felt like. Reading that book was a life changing experience for me. So much of what she wrote in the book resonated strongly with me. I learned that my mother's erratic behaviour—sometimes nice, sometimes super nasty, with no indication why it was one or the other—was not my fault. *Not my fault*. My mother most likely had Narcissistic Personality Disorder.

The only constant is change, they say, and it was time for a change. I decided that no longer would I host family dinners—holidays and birthdays and all of that. I flat out did not want my mother in my house. I had been hosting all the family dinners for about 20 years. I liked that at the time because my sons and I could be in our own house and not have to travel, like we did when I was growing up (I hated that). My sister, Jane, offered to host the family dinners, which was fine. Going to my sister's house meant that I would not have to be alone with my mother, which was when she generally made her horrid comments. No witnesses that way. I made it my mission to clean up after the meals. After dinner I cleared the table and did the dishes, leaving my mother and my sister to talk about whatever they wanted. Arm's length was as close as I wanted to be with any member of my family, in order to achieve some level of emotional safety.

My sister's experience with my mother was nothing like mine, so Jane didn't understand what I was talking about when I would tell her about it. Frankly I didn't really trust my sister either. After the PMS pill incident when I was in my 20's, I didn't see much of her, until she apologized and things went back to "normal." For her maybe, but not for me. How can you trust yourself emotionally to a person after a thing like that? There had been another incident where Jane viciously attacked me without cause. I guess she had been to a retreat of some kind and decided that I was to blame for everything that was wrong with her. I apologized for anything I said or did that may have hurt her, as hurting people was certainly not my intent. She proceeded with the cold shoulder routine, and eventually decided she was sorry and again apologized for attacking me. I always felt like the parent, and my mother and sister felt like siblings. They were all lovey and chatty, and I was ignored. It was like high school, but in my own house. It all seemed so dysfunctional.

The only person I could control was me. My mother and sister could say and do whatever they liked, and if I didn't like it, that was my problem. Speaking up and sharing that certain behaviours were hurtful just drew fire. If I hadn't done this or that then they wouldn't have said or did what they did.

My mother also said horrid things to my father from time to time, which I also didn't appreciate. As my sons didn't have a father, they didn't have a spousal relationship to observe and learn from. The only thing they had in that regard was the relationship of their grandparents. My parents' relationship was *not* the ideal relationship model I wanted for my sons. My parents sold their house and moved into a condominium, which was nice for my father as there was no yard work or snow for him to remove. In addition, I mentioned to him that with other people in the building who respected and appreciated him, mother would need to watch what she said to him and not be mean. He did say that was true, but she was still mean to him in private. When it came to narcissists, I read, no contact was the best option. For the time being, I decided on limited contact. Holidays only, and not at my house, so I could arrive and leave when I wanted. My dad opted to continue in the relationship with my mother, regardless of how mean she was to him.

One never knew which way the wind was blowing, and the following spring of 2013, my sister gave me a very extravagant gift. She had done that before. Many years ago, out of the clear blue sky, she gave me a beautiful set of silverware to go with my formal dinnerware. This time, the extravagant gift was an "exotic car tour" day. I got to drive five exotic cars through the countryside. I was *thrilled*! There was a Porsche, a Ferrari, a Nissan GTR, an Aston Martin, and a Lamborghini. *Wow.* It was a perfect day in June, and Jane offered to drive me to the car tour place. She was planning to visit her soon to be mother-in-law while I did the car tour.

Of course, I was the only woman there. The owner of the establishment told me that only 1 percent of their active drivers were women. I wore my favourite red t-shirt, jean shorts and running shoes. My sister, who looked nothing like me, wore a lovely white ruffled skirt, her hair and makeup all done up nice, nails done, fancy shoes, the whole nine yards. There were 11 men there—nine male drivers, the owner who rode the lead motorcycle, and another guy who rode the sweep motorcycle to make sure everyone stayed together. The washroom was whatever field you needed to use when we stopped to switch places/cars. I didn't drink anything all day.

I was sure all the men thought I was gay since my lovely "partner" had dropped me off. Whatever. I was me and they could think what they wanted. It had been almost 11 years since Eric died, and I was used to doing things by myself if I wanted to do them at all. There weren't many women in my martial arts class either, and I often had to work with men. Men got to do all the cool stuff, but at that point in history in this part of the world, women had lots of options. If I wanted to do something, I was going to do it. Thrive, not just survive. And thrive because of, not in spite of Eric's death. Would I have done martial arts if Eric had lived? Don't know. I'm pretty sure I would not have found myself driving a cloud-like Porsche 911 convertible, or a Ferrari F430 with intoxicating engine sounds on a perfect June day with a dude named Todd, if Eric had lived. At the end of the event day, the lead motorcycle driver told me that I drove really well. I thought I had too, but it was interesting to hear that from him. That was such an amazing day, one of the best days of my life. I felt truly alive, like I had when I rode my bicycle. I felt like anything was possible.

Yes, 2012 was over, and so was the feeling that I would like to jump out of my own skin. I moved my office to the boys' playroom, which was significantly bigger than the cubby I started with. Evan was 11 by that time, so the boys didn't play in the playroom anymore. The septic system seemed to have mended and we changed a bunch of things, like not doing all the laundry on the same day, to help it along. It was such a joy to be able to shower and do laundry in my own house. It is amazing the things we take for granted when we are no longer able to enjoy those things. I didn't understand why my sister gave me that extravagant gift, but I sure enjoyed it and was very grateful.

The Bible tells us to cast our care on God because he cares for us. I could not do anything about the septic tank, or the behaviour of my family of origin. The only thing I could do was to keep myself right, and trust God to deal with everything else. To cast my care upon him. I think I did that, and God not only sorted out the septic tank, He blessed me with a life-giving day driving amazing cars, which was a true source of hope for me that things would get better and life could still be awesome. That driving day was special to me. Not everyone would have liked that. I would not have liked it if my sister gave me the gift of a bus trip to a shopping centre in a border town. God cares for me and showed that in a way that was meaningful to me. Trust him with your cares, the things you don't like but don't have the ability to do anything about. God cares for you, and will show you in ways that are meaningful to you, when you trust Him.

PROGRESS IN SPITE
OF SETBACKS

"But those who hope in the Lord will renew their strength. They will soar on wings like eagles; they will run and not grow weary, they will walk and not be faint" (Isaiah 40:31 NIV).

The year Greg turned 16, he wanted to get a job. The family of his friend from school owned the local lumberyard, and told Greg they were hiring. I helped Greg with his resume, and he got the job. The first weekend, he worked at a water softener salt sale. I don't know how many hundred pounds of salt he lugged that weekend, but he was sore. Added to my duties was taking Greg to and from work. The nice thing about the hardware store job was that it was across the street from his high school, so he just walked over to work after school. They closed at six, so there were never late nights there, and we could still get to our martial arts classes, which meant he could keep doing his own classes and teaching the younger kids.

I had taught all the boys to ride bicycles, and the next lesson was driving. Greg was a good driver and he mastered the manual transmission fairly quickly. He successfully passed his driver's test and was able to buy himself a truck with the money he had saved from his lumberyard job. I didn't know about old used trucks, so a gentleman from our martial arts school, who was a car guy, went with us to look at a truck. He said it would be a good one, so Greg bought it. Of course, it needed work. The son of one of our friends from church was a mechanic's apprentice, so he and Greg worked together to do what needed to be done so the truck would pass the safety test. That was a great learning opportunity for both boys. Now Greg could drive himself to and from work. When he would go out with his friends or his girlfriend, he would come and visit with me for an hour or so before going off to bed. It was so wonderful to see my precious son, who was growing up without a dad, doing so well.

Kyle was in high school, and he had been accepted into a special program for high IQ kids in a neighbouring town. He didn't qualify for busing as it was a special program and not regular school. Since we lived on the highway between the two towns, there was no city bus service. Another student from Kyle's eighth grade class was in the same program, so we were able to carpool, which was really nice. I was on pick up duty, so every day around 3:00 pm I drove to the next city to collect the boys and drive the "carpool kid" home. I was very grateful that Kyle had a ride to school in the morning.

In our area, students in ninth grade have a day in the school year where they go to their parent's workplace for the day. I already had Kyle doing some data entry for me, so there didn't seem like much of an advantage for him to shadow my work for the day.

Our friend's daughter was studying for her master's in physics at the University that Kyle wanted to attend, so we arranged for Kyle to have a tour of the laser lab she worked in for "take your kid to work" day. The university was about 45 minutes from our house, very close to where I grew up. I could take him to the lab for the afternoon because I mostly worked from home.

Kyle loved the school and made it his mission to go to that university.

Evan was in middle school around that time. He had written a book, a quest of sorts. We found something online which allowed him to format his book and have it printed and bound. He did the artwork for the cover himself. I think we had ten books printed. It was a cute little story. He worked diligently through the whole process and was quite pleased that he had become a published author at the age of 12.

In addition to literature, Evan was also interested in music and drama. He wanted to learn how to play the guitar, and we got him a ¾ guitar so he could get his little hand around the neck of the guitar. His guitar teacher helped him with a piece of music that Evan practiced so he could perform at the school's talent show. In the end, playing the guitar took more work than Evan wanted, so the guitar lessons stopped.

Evan was the lead actor in the school play one year as well. Lots of people from church went to see the play, as their children also went to that school. Evan received several compliments on his performance in the play. One year, the enrichment school program he attended was having a field trip to the Stratford Festival. There were several theatres there, and the main stage was reserved for Shakespearean plays. William Shatner and Christopher Plummer performed there when they were starting out their acting careers in the 1950's, so it was pretty exciting to have the opportunity to go there and see a play. In addition to seeing the play, Evan and his class had the opportunity to go through a costume area and do some improv on the actual stage wearing the costumes they selected.

My business was doing well and I was gaining more clients through referrals. Being able to choose when I worked, and being available to pick Kyle up from school in the next city and take the guys to martial arts was such an amazing blessing. Somehow, by the grace of God, the money I made doing that work was enough, and we had everything we needed. People would sometimes say, "You have four sons, right?"

I would say, "No, I only have three, it just sounds like four." Our house was loud and busy all the time, but I did love it. I loved having sons.

I taught all the guys how to cook because they were *always* hungry. I decided it would free up some of my time if they could make their own food. Kyle took to cooking and asked if he could cook the meals instead of helping with the clean up. Sounded like a deal to me. We decided what the menu would be and he cooked the food. It worked out really well. It was fun for me to be in my office and wait to hear that the meal was being served. Only a short time prior, it was me telling him to come for supper. It was truly amazing how quickly things were moving forward for all of us.

For Kyle's 13th birthday, I took him to see *The War Horse* at a theatre about an hour away. It was a play, and the horse was a puppet which was operated by three puppeteers. We had awesome seats and it was a really great event. I loved being with my sons and doing things that they enjoyed with them. It gave me such joy to see them enjoying themselves, having my undivided attention.

When Greg was in grade 11, he opted to do a full day co-op with a fence and deck contractor for the one semester.

The contractor was a friend of a friend from church. Greg learned a lot, which was wonderful on many levels, the main one being the family cottage—the one my grandfather had built, and that I had gone to almost every year of my life, as had my sons. My parents wanted to sell the cottage. Greg and I were devastated. I asked God, "If there is any way for me to have this cottage, I would love to have it."

In the coming weeks, a friend emailed me to say that I had been on her mind, and that if I had a financial decision to make, to go for it, because my situation would be changing, and it would work out okay. I was blown away that she would say that to me. Then another friend drove an hour from her house and showed up at my house one day to say that she thought I should borrow the money and just buy the cottage. She also said that my situation would change, and that if worse came to worst, I could just sell the cottage. I told my mother it would be very sad for my sons and I to never be able to go to the cottage again. Her snarky reply was, "Unless you can quickly marry someone who has money and is good at fixing things, this is how it has to be."

I looked into borrowing some money, and bought the cottage, which my mother inherited, even though she kept increasing the price and shortening the time I had to put everything together. I believed that the price increases and shortened closing dates were her attempt to ensure that I would fail in my quest to purchase the family cottage. I went through my lawyer to ensure everything was done correctly, which stopped the price increases. My mother told me that she would "give me a different price" if I would tell her where I was getting the money from, which I did not do. That offer left me feeling like I was being controlled. It seemed that she believed she had the power to change the price and the closing date at her whim, which she offered to change if I would give her what she wanted—the source of my funding. The closing date was my mother's birthday, June 30, 2014.

My funding came through, and that day I became the sole owner of my family cottage. I was beside myself with joy and gratitude. And also fear. How in the world would I be able to pay that back? The fact that the funding came through and the deal closed properly with lawyers involved was a miracle! I would need more miracles to pay the loan back and do the upkeep at two properties. But I had made it this far despite difficulties and obstacles. Rather than be afraid, I decided to enjoy my cottage and look forward to more awesome things happening in the future.

My dad couldn't keep up with the work at the cottage, so it needed lots of work. A friend referred me to a retired gentleman who was able to help with a major repair that summer. I went to the cottage with the boys and met our contractor there. Greg helped him, and he said that if he was still in business he would hire Greg in a heartbeat as they were able to get more done than he had hoped in the time allotted. I was so profoundly grateful for Greg and that he was able to help with that project, and so very proud of him as well. I was profoundly grateful that out of our whole family, my beloved cottage was mine!

When Greg was in grade 12, he agreed that he would like to become a plumber like his father, his grandfather, and his uncle. He had his dad's personality and skill set, so I knew he would be great at that job. The trouble was, it was hard to get an apprenticeship without any experience. The school was not helpful for people who were trade minded, so I was on my own. Again. Thankfully, there was Google. I searched for apprenticeship related things and found a private pre-apprenticeship training school, which was about a 30 minute drive from where we lived. I spoke to the admissions officer on the phone and booked a tour. Greg loved it. We signed him up for the plumbing and gas program.

The student would either need a grade 12 education or have to pass an equivalency test. Since Greg was in grade 12 at the time, he did the equivalency test and passed. We had some insurance money saved after Eric's death, so we used that for the tuition. Greg was busy. He did the pre-apprenticeship program in the morning, high school in the afternoon, and went to his lumberyard job after school. I did the best I could to help him manage all of that, which was a lot for an 18 year old guy. It took nine months for him to complete both programs, so only a few months were while he was still in high school. In the summer and fall he did the program in the morning and worked at the lumberyard in the afternoon, almost every day. They loved him at the lumberyard and it was a great job. They had him driving the delivery truck as soon as he got his driver's license. He dealt with business owners and construction workers all day, which he was very good at because of his personality, and because of the leadership training he had done in martial arts. Part of that training was to speak to parents about how their kids were doing in class, so Greg was really comfortable speaking with adults.

That year, Greg turned 18. He was finishing high school, miraculously. When he was six years old, he wanted a Cloud City Star Wars Lego set. It was $150, so I said no. I thought it would go on sale or whatever, and I could get it later. I was so wrong about that. Lego only made a certain number of each set they created, so when they were gone, that was it. The Lego sets skyrocketed in value. Greg hated school, but I knew it was of the utmost importance that he get his grade 12 done. I managed to find a Cloud City Star Wars Lego set online at $900! I bought the set and told him he could have it *when* he finished high school, and that if he didn't finish, I'd sell it for more than I paid for it and life would go on. I showed him the box and he touched it as if it were fine silk. Then I hid it in a locked closet. Greg finished high school and received his long-awaited Cloud City Star Wars Lego set.

The Bible tells us that when we wait upon the Lord our strength will be renewed. That we will soar on wings like eagles, that we will run and not grow weary. I saw that truth play out in my life in spades during that part of my life. Being a single parent with three sons is one thing, having two of them be teenagers was something else. I constantly felt like I was on a high speed treadmill, and I knew it wouldn't be long before all three of the boys would be teenagers. Joyce Meyer says that we are partners with God. That we *can't* do God's part and He *won't* do our part. My part was to get up every day and do what needed to be done with the goal of providing my sons with resources and opportunities for success. God's part was to renew my strength so I could keep up. It was a beautiful partnership.

GRATITUDE

"No one will be able to stand against you all the days of your life. As I was with Moses, so I will be with you; I will never leave you or forsake you" (Joshua 1:5 NIV).

That spring, it was time to open the cottage. Greg had helped my dad with that the year before, so he knew how to get the well and pump going, as well as the rest of the opening procedure. By then a couple of Greg's friends also had trucks. They were 18, and they wanted to open the cottage on the long weekend in May. They also said they would tear down a bad section of deck and rebuild it, which Greg knew how to do because he had worked with a fence and deck contractor the year before. The idea of letting five 18-year old guys be at a cottage unsupervised on a long weekend seemed like a very bad idea. That being said, Greg had been friends with these guys since kindergarten and I had watched them go from five year olds to 18 year olds. They had all been at our house many times, and Greg had been to their houses many times, so I also knew all the boys' parents. Greg had been in a leadership role at the martial arts school for many years. He was strong, brave, confident, and clear about his expectations. He loved the cottage as much as I did and I told him if they messed up this chance they would never go again.

Greg and I discussed that at length, and I finally relented. He made a materials list and I ordered everything from the lumberyard near the cottage. I paid for it over the phone, and the yard would deliver everything. To complicate matters, the cottage had no road access, so Greg and his friends had to ferry all the wood across the river on our trusty old pontoon boat. They opened the cottage, rebuilt the section of deck, and were very responsible. Everything worked out. I was grateful and proud of Greg and his friends, and they were thrilled to be trusted with such a task.

One of Greg's friends went on to be a mechanic, and another did roofing for several summers while he was in school. Over the next several years, the guys replaced another section of deck, and the roof, among many other smaller jobs. They now continue to open and close the cottage, and spend a long weekend there in the summer as well. They also bring their girlfriends. Two of the guys started a podcast, which I have been listening to, as I have known all these guys since they were in kindergarten, and it is so wonderful to see what amazing men they have become. I thought it interesting that the two podcast guys were discussing starting a podcast on one of their "cottage trips."

Greg went on to get a job at a plumbing company which specialized in well and septic. Perfect! If the well and/or septic at the cottage needed service, Greg could manage that.

Kyle landed a full-time summer job for two summers while he was in high school. The plan was for him to save his money and buy himself a car, so he could drive himself to school. Since Kyle didn't have a friend who was a mechanic's apprentice to help him fix up his car, we found one that had already passed the safety check and was ready to drive away. Kyle's driver's test was the first day of school, and he simply had to pass the first time. Since the place we bought the car was about a half hour away, and since Kyle didn't have his driver's license yet as it was early in August, we needed another driver to drive Kyle's car back home. Our friend's son was 18 and had his license, so he came with us to pick up the car.

Kyle's "new" car was a real beater. It was a tan Chevrolet Malibu. Tan inside and out. Part of the letters on "Malibu" on the trunk of the car were missing, so Kyle began to call his new treasure the "solid gold Malible." The car was a serious mess inside, so we rented an upholstery shampooing machine from the local hardware store, and Kyle spent a weekend shampooing the seats in his car. They came up surprisingly well. He was still working his summer job and I would drive him to work in his car, and when I picked him up after work, I did so in his car and he would drive home. All he had to do next was to pass his driver's test on the first day of school, which he did! This freed up more time for me to take on more bookkeeping clients and earn more money.

That summer Evan wanted to go to a basketball day camp. That was in a city about a half hour away. Thankfully the camp was only a week long. At that point all the boys were teenagers, and taking Evan to basketball camp in another city ramped things up into a seriously high gear as far as the single parent treadmill was concerned. Kyle started work at eight, so I took him to work. The week of basketball camp, I would go back to the house, pick up Evan and drive him to basketball camp a half hour away, half an hour back home, and then start working. Basketball camp went from 9am-3pm, so at 2:30pm, I would leave to get Evan and be back by 3:30pm, just in time to pick Kyle up from work at 4:00. I was happy to do it because Evan needed things to do, and he wanted to try out for the rep basketball team in the fall, so some extra training and practice with basketball seemed like a good idea. My main goal was to help my sons be successful and not miss out on any opportunities just because they didn't have a dad.

Evan had been accepted into the same special program at Kyle's high school, so that fall he was in ninth grade while Kyle was in twelfth. Kyle drove both of them to school in the "solid gold Malible," so I didn't have to do any of that. Kyle cooked the meals.

The Bible tells us that God will never leave us or forsake us, and that He will always be with us, and that no one will be able to stand against us. I knew that was true because I felt like there was no other way I would have been able to do all the things I did that summer, right down to my work, which allowed me to drive Kyle to work and Evan to day camp. To be able to get all my work done for my clients, and enjoy time at *my* cottage with my sons. I was deeply and profoundly grateful for how things were progressing for all of us, and that things just always seemed to work out.

A NEW MINDSET

"But he said to me, 'my grace is sufficient for you for my power is made perfect in weakness'" (2 Cor 12:9 NIV).

My friend from college often came to visit. She was a sales rep and sometimes her territory was the area near my house on the highway, so she would stop by for a tea after her rounds were complete. In November, after we closed our newly purchased family cottage for the first time, my friend dropped in.

I always thought of Rob on his birthday. I noticed that when I thought of Rob over the years, I wasn't angry about what had happened anymore. I had been thinking about him, and curious about what had become of him. My curiosity led me to creep on his Facebook page.

I discovered he was also living in Two Rivers, which seriously freaked me out. Two Rivers was a small town, like 10,000 people, so it was just a matter of time before I saw him at the grocery store or hardware store or something. I showed my friend Rob's Facebook page. She remembered him from our college days, as he and I had still been dating at that time. Thirty years had gone by. Her comment was that he was a good-looking man.

I don't know what happened in my brain, but I sent him a private Facebook message. I guess I thought that I would rather connect with him behind the safety of my keyboard than run into him at a store and connect with him in person after 30 years and a lot of water under the bridge. In my mind, speaking with him online would give me control over the situation, or time to think about what I would say, at least. Why I cared about running into him in a store, I don't know. In any case, I sent him a private message. I kept it generic, like I would to anyone else I was friends with in high school that I had discovered moved away from where we grew up and was now living in Two Rivers, like me. So that is what I sent: "What brought you to Two Rivers?" or something like that.

At that time, once or twice a week I was walking the indoor track at the local sports complex with a friend. We did many laps, which was nice because it was winter and always cold, dark, and snowy outside. I told my friend that I had creeped Rob's Facebook page and sent him a private message, and that I hadn't heard back from him. I didn't know what to make of that. I guess I just would have to deal with it if I ran into him in town somewhere.

By then, Joe, our beloved martial arts instructor, had sold the martial arts school and moved away. The new ownership was very nice, but it just wasn't the same. Since the older boys had aged out of the program and we didn't really like the new curriculum, Evan asked if he could play basketball and ball hockey. So basketball and ball hockey it was. Of course, in ball hockey he wanted to be the goalie, and ball hockey gear was more cost effective than ice hockey gear. Still, Evan really loved hockey and jerseys and music. His favourite team was the Chicago Blackhawks. For Evan's 13th birthday, we went to see an NHL game. I couldn't take him to Chicago, as that was a nine-hour drive. But the Blackhawks were going to be playing in Buffalo, which was only about an hour from where we lived.

He went online and chose the seats, which were ten rows behind the goalie. We went and got passports because we would be coming from Canada. The day finally came. As it turned out, that game was on a Friday. Good Friday, in fact. So with it being a holiday and a long weekend, the traffic crossing the border was ridiculous. I had wanted to take him to a restaurant for some Buffalo style wings, but we didn't have time, not if we were going to make the hockey game. The game was the point of going, so we opted to just go to Wendy's for a burger instead.

Buffalo was doing very poorly that year, so the game was more like a Chicago home game than a Buffalo home game. There were a *lot* of Chicago fans there, and Evan was wearing the Chicago jersey he'd received for Christmas the year before. When Chicago scored, the place erupted. It was really exciting and fun.

It took us a long time to get back across the border, as the traffic was really heavy. By the time we got home it was about 2:00 am. But it was a Friday night and I was so delighted to spend that time with my youngest son, enjoying the things he enjoyed.

Evan also made the rep team for basketball when he was 14. There were practices multiple times per week, and the games were mostly tournaments. We travelled here and there, stayed in hotels, and did the tournament thing. His brothers were older and could manage at home fine by themselves. We went back to Buffalo for a basketball tournament. In one tournament, there were several hours between games, so we went to see a movie of Evan's choice, which was fun. I loved being with him.

Ball hockey was also fun. It was just a house league in town, so it was only 15 minutes to get there. He was an amazing goalie. He was tall and handsome—I know, I have a biased opinion—and it was something to see the girls on the team swoon over him. My precious little boy, surrounded by giggling girls. All my sons were growing up and becoming men. Soon I would be by myself. Then what?

I developed pneumonia in the winter of 2015, the week before Christmas. I have no idea where I got it from, but thankfully I got over that in a couple of months. January and February were my busiest months with work, so being taken out by pneumonia was not ideal. The church budget for that year had to be approved by the board and finalized by the end of January. Many of my other clients had sales tax returns due at the end of January as well. The prior business year for the church needed to be complete and to the accountant by the end of January so he could do his work and have the reports ready for the annual meeting in February. February was also really busy because the rest of my clients had tax filing deadlines, forms to be issued, and year ends sent to accountants for tax preparation. Because of the pneumonia, I could only work for half a day before needing a nap. I think all I did for those two months was work and sleep. By the end of February I could actually make it through a whole day without a nap. When diagnosed by the doctor at Christmas, he said it would take me two months to get over the pneumonia. He was exactly right. I was glad he told me the timeline so I understood that when I was tired I needed to rest. No high speed single parent treadmill during that time.

Between running kids around and martial arts and everything, it had been many years since I rode my bicycle. I decided in the summer of 2016 that I would try riding my old mountain bike, the one Eric bought me when we moved to Two Rivers, just to see if my lungs still worked after the pneumonia. I rode all over town, visited my friends, and checked out the trail network. My lungs worked! It had been over 20 years since Eric had given me that bike. I could tell, as I was not the same rider I was the first time I rode the bike. The bike had not aged, but I had. It was interesting that a gift he gave me over 20 years ago was again being enjoyed. So much had happened in my life since my bicycle riding days. Eric had been gone for 14 years at that point, and I noticed that I looked on the bicycle and being able to ride it, not with sadness that he was gone, but rather with gratitude that I had spent that time with him, and that he had cared enough about what was important to me to give me that bicycle.

A friend from church was part of a bicycle club in a neighbouring city, so I asked her about her bicycle and the club and how it all worked. I had been saving my birthday and Christmas money for several years, and decided that the following spring, I would buy a new bicycle and join the bicycle club. That seemed like a great plan, now that I knew my lungs worked after the pneumonia. That way I could ride and not be by myself (there is safety in numbers), and maybe meet some new people, since I wouldn't be hanging out with my sons anymore as they were growing up and moving on. I was 100 percent devoted to those boys and put everything I had into helping them grow into successful men. Consequently, I didn't see much of my friends. Anyway, none of my friends were into cycling, except that one from church. Besides, it was a couple's world, and I wasn't a couple, so that limited the hanging out with my friends to a certain degree. Everyone was busy as well.

Rob had still not responded to the private message I sent him, and I wasn't sure what to make of that. Maybe he had forgotten all about me. Maybe he was angry because I had been mean to him on more than one occasion. Maybe he moved away from Two Rivers and didn't see the point in responding. Maybe I would run into him at the grocery store, or the bank, and have to add to that potential conversation the awkwardness of him not responding to my message.

March has always been a tricky month for me. The anniversary of Eric's death and his birthday were both in March, so I usually spent the majority of the month thinking about Eric and my experiences since his death. The spring of 2017 marked the 15th anniversary of his death. Greg had a full-time job as an apprentice, Kyle would be going away to university in the fall, and Evan only had two years of high school left. I'd been on a fast-moving single parent treadmill for 15 years, and that was finally starting to wind down. Besides growing my business and riding my bicycle in a club one night a week, what would I do with myself? I was extremely proud of all my sons and all they were accomplishing. I was proud of me, too. I never quit nor gave up and kept pressing forward. The time was coming for me to reinvent myself, again.

In the Bible, Paul talks about having a thorn in his flesh. We aren't sure what that is, whether it is physical or emotional, or something else entirely. All we know is that he doesn't like it and asks God to take it away from him. But God doesn't take it away. He just says that His grace is sufficient, and that His power is made perfect in our weakness. I was beginning to understand that. The "thorn" in my flesh was the fact that

Eric had died and I was raising three boys by myself. I would have preferred to not go through that, to not have to deal with that kind of a thorn, which is why I appreciated that verse so much. God's power *is* made perfect in our weakness. I had tremendous weakness, sometimes more than others, like having pneumonia and not being able to function for a whole day. It was always amazing to see how God could make things work through his limitless strength when my weakness threatened to overtake me.

A NEW HOPE

"He who is able to do immeasurably more than all we ask or imagine..." (Eph 3:20 NIV).

I was coming up on the 15th anniversary of Eric's death. Fifteen years of the high-speed single parent treadmill. Fifteen years of my sons not knowing their dad and growing up without him. Fifteen years of wondering how our lives would have been had Eric not died. Fifteen years of just barely enough to get by. Fifteen years of nobody completely knowing my whole, authentic self, and truly loving me anyway. Many years prior, I had accepted the fact that Eric was gone, and I just had to get on with it and did the best I could with what I had. I wondered if there was a man out there, besides Eric, who could actually love me.

Eric, and all my sons, loved Star Wars. If you're a Star Wars fan, you know that the very first Star Wars movie ever was called *A New Hope*. The Oxford dictionary defines hope as "a feeling of expectation and a desire for a certain thing to happen."

I had been *hoping* to meet a wonderful man who would completely know my whole, authentic self, and truly love me anyway. It had been over ten years since I dabbled in dating. I had decided that dating was a waste of my time, that I would be much better off investing myself and my time in my sons and their growth and development than on some prince who would ultimately be revealed as a frog. Many years ago, God asked me, "If you never get married again, will you still serve me?" I immediately answered *Yes*. I could live without a husband, but I could not live without God. He was always there, always available, every second of every night and every day. *He* knew my whole, authentic self, and truly loved me anyway. He was faithful. He made the impossible possible. After all, I was still living in the house I loved on the highway. And I was the sole owner of my beloved family cottage. I was convinced that none other than God could have made those things possible. Not to mention the thousands of other small, daily victories I had experienced in my life, specifically in the past 15 years.

I interpreted that question, "If you never get married again, will you still serve me?" to mean that I was destined to be alone for the rest of my life. In some ways, part of me believed that if I hadn't married Eric, I wouldn't be in the situation I was in, so it was my own fault. Which was ridiculous. For starters, if I had not married Eric and had done something else, things might be worse. And I did have my precious sons, a lovely home, my beloved cottage, vibrant, dynamic health, amazing friends, and the promise that God can use *all* things for good. I lived in a part of the world where women are taken seriously and have a voice. I had resources and opportunities. In spite of things not being perfect, I was deeply and profoundly grateful for what I did have. God had been in the habit of giving me the desires of my heart over the years, so I had *hope* that someday, somehow, there was actually a wonderful man out there who would truly love me.

Maybe once all the boys were grown up, had moved on with their lives, and I was no longer on the high-speed treadmill of being a single parent.

Technology is a funny thing, and God has a delightful sense of humour. I had never been a fan of social media, and yet, one day in early March 2017, shortly after the 15th anniversary of Eric's death, it happened. I received a message on Facebook. It was Rob. I had messaged him on Facebook two years and four months earlier. It seemed the message had been floating in cyberspace all that time and he had just received it. He was inquiring if it was actually me that sent the message, or if there was some hacking going on somewhere. I confirmed that it was indeed me who had sent that message. It was hard for both of us to believe that it took two years and four months to reach him.

Rob proceeded to apologize profusely for how things had gone between us some 30 years ago. I had been wronged by lots of people over the years, as we all are, however, I was not accustomed to hearing apologies. In fact, whenever I had told my mother that her behaviour was hurting me, she would blame me for her behaviour. That was the exact opposite of an apology, in my opinion. I was very intrigued by Rob's words. He invited me to continue the "conversation," but said he totally understood if I wanted nothing to do with him.

Keep in mind these were all private Facebook messages—the only tone was in the writing. No actual voice or anything. The tone from his writing left me feeling like he had been holding his breath for 30 years, and finally had the chance to exhale. I found that very intriguing, and decided that since I didn't have to worry about a husband wondering why I was communicating with my high school boyfriend, that I would be interested to hear what else Rob had to say. I knew from his Facebook profile that he was living in Two Rivers, which was why I messaged him in the first place. I preferred to be proactive rather than reactive, which was why I sent him a message two years and four months earlier. I decided that if I could get these types of pleasantries out of the way when I had the opportunity to censor and edit my responses, that would suit me better than running into him somewhere and having to figure that out on the fly.

Also, I was acutely aware of how much I had changed in those 30 years. I was still me, but the school of hard knocks had worn off a few rough edges. I expected that might be true for Rob as well.

So I said I was okay to continue exchanging private messages with him on Facebook Messenger. I was curious about what the last 30 years had been like for him, but I was also heavily guarded, and was grateful for being able to communicate behind the safety of my keyboard.

We sent a message or two every day about this and that. I learned that Rob's love for cars had resulted in him becoming a mechanic, that he had been divorced and was not in a relationship at that time. Rob knew through the paper that Eric had died 15 years earlier. Only a few days of messaging had passed, and Rob asked me if I was in a relationship with anyone. Somehow, I knew that question was coming. I also knew that Rob's father was an atheist, and Rob had identified as that as well, when we were young.

At that point in my life, God was everything to me, so I was sure that if I told him that he would start running for the hills. So I told him I was in a relationship of sorts with Jesus. That I was, in fact, a "Jesus freak." Interestingly, he didn't abruptly end the conversation. In fact, he began to ask a lot of questions about my relationship with Jesus. I very boldly told him exactly what I thought, and why. I felt like he wanted to be in a relationship with me, but I was quite happy by myself, and was planning on waiting a few more years before I mired myself in dating, when the boys would be adults and self-sufficient then. Besides, we had played the on again/off again game in our youth and I certainly wasn't interested in starting that up again.

I began to look forward to the images of coffee Rob started sending in the morning. Every day when I checked my device, there was a lovely picture of a steaming cup of coffee, with warm wishes for a nice day. I would respond with gratitude for the lovely message, a happy face emoji and wish him well that day too. Soon after, he also started sending a picture of some flowers. I could feel myself being drawn to him. In science fiction terms, I was caught in a tractor beam and I fought that with everything I had. I told God that I could not endure being strung along and left heartbroken, to help me understand my feelings and to please help me put an end to the messaging before someone got hurt.

One snowy Sunday afternoon, a couple of weeks into our messaging, we spent the entire afternoon messaging. Playful banter, clever comments, poking fun the way close friends do. It was really fun, until it wasn't. I forget how it came up, but Rob may have invited me to ask him anything, and that he would answer it honestly. So I asked him. I asked him about the various things that happened in our relationship when we were young, the things that broke my heart into a million pieces, the things I didn't see coming and couldn't understand why they happened. Things that caused me to doubt that I was worth loving. I asked some very difficult questions that left me in tears. It was odd how 30 years had passed, and I had experienced so much life since then, but I was suddenly 17 again, with my heart broken into a million pieces.

I was extremely grateful to be asking those questions behind the safety of my keyboard. He had no idea how my asking those questions had affected me. I suppose I had no idea how asking those questions affected him either. In any case, he answered the questions. All of them. Basically, he said he was young and stupid and didn't appreciate what he had with me until it was gone. That there was no one like me. I suspected that whatever I said on the day I spun my tires and drove away like a maniac may have struck a chord as well. I never did remember what I said that day, and he was reluctant to tell me, although he did share that I said I wished I had never met him and wasted four years of my life with him.

I was not accustomed to that kind of response when telling someone how their behaviour affected me. Eric was a good man. Both of us had controlling mothers. I think that whenever he and I disagreed on something, he felt like I was trying to control him, but I was just trying to understand and explain how his behaviour affected me. I knew what it felt like to be controlled, and I did *not* want to do that to someone else. At the end of the day, I had very poor skills with managing conflict and just didn't do it well. Hard conversations with Eric just left me feeling far away from him.

Having that hard conversation with Rob, and his answers to my questions, left me feeling closer to him. I felt sure that this was God's answer to my query. It was Rob who opened that can of worms. I knew that I was not being strung along, only to be left heartbroken. I had asked God to help me put a stop to the messaging with Rob before someone got hurt, but it seemed like the messaging brought some closure and some healing from things that happened in my youth that I didn't understand, rather than hurt and distrust. It was all very moving and felt impossible.

We messaged a bit more about Jesus, and I was concerned that Rob was just telling me what I wanted to hear, so I suggested he speak with my pastor. He said he would. Saying he would and actually meeting with the pastor were two different things, in my mind. I was sure that would be the end of it. At least I had some answers, and something positive to say about the demise of our teenage romance.

I spoke to my pastor about Rob. I told him briefly that we had been high school sweethearts, and the relationship hadn't ended well. That we had reconnected after 30 years, and that Rob had some questions about God that I thought would be better answered by him. Pastor Jeff said to give Rob his contact information, as he preferred people to contact him in cases like that. I did that, and Rob told me he had scheduled time to meet Jeff for coffee. The daily pics of coffee and flowers from Rob continued, and we continued to message. I continued to look forward to our messaging time, but was also concerned I was getting in over my head. In any case, I felt I could say *anything* to Rob. We had a lot of history together, really knew each other, and I was determined to be 100 percent authentic about everything, all the time. If he didn't like it, he could go on with his life and leave me alone.

Rob told me about his meeting with Pastor Jeff. I called Pastor Jeff and told him I knew he couldn't tell me what he and Rob had talked about, but could he at least tell me if he believed Rob's interest in God was sincere? Pastor Jeff believed that Rob was sincere in his quest to learn more about God. I flat out would *not* be in a relationship with someone who did not share my faith, and here was the atheist, sincerely wanting to learn about God, which I found rather shocking. What else had changed about Rob in 30 years? I was desperately curious to find out, but I was afraid that I would get sucked in and be sorry I went down that path. He was, at that time, the way he was when we first met at McDonald's all those years ago. My heart was melting, and the idea of picking up where we left off when things were good was intoxicating, and probably impossible. The inner dialogue between my emotions and powers of reason was relentless. They say a leopard doesn't change its spots. So, was the Rob I was experiencing now the Rob I met when I was 15? Or was the on again/off again Rob the real Rob?

Still looking for other ways to get out of this tangle I found myself in, I contacted Pastor John, a retired minister. He had baptized all my sons and buried Eric. I had known him for 20 years and he was like a father to me, my go-to person for advice and support when navigating my life became tricky. I went to John's house and told him about Rob and our history, and about what was happening then. John never told me what to do, he just gave me different ways to think about things. Like, what if a relationship with him works out, would I love that? And what if I kick him to the curb? Will I wonder what might have been for the rest of my life? Ultimately, after speaking with Pastor John, I felt like I should proceed with caution as far as Rob was concerned. So, proceed I did.

Somewhere along the line in my single parent journey, I thought it would be nice to someday be in a wonderful relationship with a lovely man. I had made a list of the things I would like in a partner. I wrote it all down, and then promptly threw the list in the garbage. First of all, I figured there wasn't a man on earth who would have all of those qualities, so I might as well stay happy being alone. Secondly, if something happened to me, I wouldn't want people to be going through my stuff and seeing this weird list of desirable qualities in a man.

The Bible tells us in Ephesians 3:20 that God is able to do immeasurably more than we could ask or imagine. Even though I had thrown out my list of desirable qualities in a man, I still remembered the qualities I admired. I began to notice that Rob had *all* of those qualities. And then some. Rob was immeasurably more than I could ask or imagine. Instead of being afraid of getting hurt, I began to look forward to seeing him and spending time with him to get a closer look at the man he had become.

BEYOND MY WILDEST DREAMS

"I will repay you for the years the locusts have eaten--" (Joel 2:25a NIV).

On Tuesdays I worked at a client's office, which I did not have the wifi password for. Back then, I didn't have data on my phone, so I couldn't get any messenger messages unless I was at home. I insisted on using messenger, rather than giving Rob my cell number for texting, so I had more control over how he could connect with me. I reasoned that if things went wrong, I could delete my Facebook profile, which I never posted on anyway, and that would be the end of it. Somehow, I still received a messenger message from Rob while I was at that office. He invited me to meet him for tea at Tim Hortons. I accepted his invitation, and my message was sent. As soon as I sent the message accepting Rob's invitation, "You're the Inspiration" by Chicago came on the radio. That was "our song" from our youth. The lady I was assisting in the office was a lovely Christian woman, and at that moment I became quite emotional, so I decided to tell her what was going on since she was concerned about me. She was thrilled, and offered to pray for me as I moved deeper into the abyss.

Until then, I hadn't told anyone about what was happening except for the two pastors.

My tea date at Tim Hortons arrived. I wore my favourite jeans and the Rothmans Porsche t-shirt I bought at the racetrack when Rob and I went there over 30 years ago. It was a very special t-shirt, so I only wore it once or twice a year as I wanted it to stay nice. I brought the photo album I had kept, of pictures of us from our youth.

I was there a good half hour before Rob was to arrive. I wanted to watch him come in rather than having him watch me come in. I also wanted to buy my own tea. He arrived sooner than I expected, and I didn't see him come in. I heard a voice behind me say, "There's a face I haven't seen in a long time." My heart jumped. I knew it was Rob. I got out of my seat and hugged him because that felt like a normal thing to do. I hugged my friends and my sons after all. He went and got his tea, and we set about speaking in person, after 30 years of being apart and several weeks of corresponding via Facebook Messenger. I showed him the photo album because I was interested in his response to the photos. It was a very nostalgic time. Rob sat across the table from me and ended up holding my hand in both of his hands. When we were young, our hands were almost the same size. Now, he had big, strong, rough man hands, and mine looked very small by comparison. His hands had matured. What else about Rob had matured? He looked absolutely overcome with joy, and I was astonished that he really had wanted to be with me for all of those years. I think he was astonished that I still had my Rothmans Porsche t-shirt, which he remembered me purchasing.

Our tea date came to an end, and we decided to go out to a movie that weekend. He walked me to my car, and hugged me before I got in my car and drove away. It was the most magical time I had ever spent drinking tea at Tim Hortons.

That weekend, we went to see *The Shack*. The movie was playing in a theatre about 45 minutes from my home. We met at the church parking lot, and I drove. I wanted to drive because...I wanted to drive. I had been to see the movie the weekend before with a friend. My friend and I had both read the book. The movie was brilliant and brought us both to tears. When Rob suggested we see a movie, I suggested *The Shack*, because I wanted to see what he thought of the movie and discuss it with him. It was a very moving story and I thought his reaction at the emotional parts of the movie—which I knew of, and he didn't—would tell me more about him. It was the story of a man who had an encounter with God that changed his life.

Rob found *The Shack* to be quite a moving story as well. We went out for tea afterwards. When we were young, Rob always had a moustache. Over the 30 years where we had gone our separate ways, he still had a moustache, but it was seriously out of control. I had said to God that I didn't like the moustache. Still looking for ways to get out of being in a relationship with him, I guess. That evening, while drinking tea after watching *The Shack*, Rob asked for my opinion about his moustache—the very objection I had to being with him which I had discussed with God. For crying out loud! I knew how much he loved his moustache, but I told him I didn't like it because it hid his dimples. Aside from feeling a bit awkward about having to answer that question, we had a very lovely evening.

We drove back to Two Rivers, and I dropped him off at his car in the church parking lot. We had a lovely hug, and I think the thought of kissing me crossed his mind, but his crazy moustache wouldn't allow for that.

Easter was coming up, so I invited Rob to come to the Good Friday evening service at our church. He could enter by that door, and sit back there, and I would sit where I normally sat. He was nervous about that, but attended the service. Good Friday service was always very moving. Afterward, we met at Tim Hortons for tea.

From what I understood, Rob discussed the moustache, and me, with his mother. She remembered me from our youth when I would spend time at their house. Rob decided to entirely remove the moustache by the next time I saw him. He was dashingly handsome, and I could see his dimples. To say I was shocked would be an understatement. I had *never* seen him without a moustache, and I knew how much he loved it. The fact that he took such a bold step spoke volumes to me about what he thought about my opinion. I just said I didn't like the moustache because it hid his dimples. I didn't ask him to get rid of it. I just thought a reasonable moustache, rather than one he could tie under his chin, might be in order.

Our next time together we went to visit his mother. The boys asked me where I was going, and I told them I was going to have tea with a friend. Greg said I'd been out for tea an awful lot lately, and asked what exactly was going on. I told him I was actually going on a date, and his response was, "Oh yeah? Who is this klutz?"

"His name is Rob."

"Wasn't your high school boyfriend's name Rob?"

Greg's response left me seriously flustered. Greg and I always had a special relationship, but somehow he seemed to know exactly what was going on.

"Yes, the high school boyfriend's name was Rob."

"Where did you meet this guy?" Greg asked.

"When I was out," I answered.

"But you don't look at people or talk to them when you are out," Greg protested.

I don't think I said anything. I don't remember exactly what happened, but I believe I confirmed to Greg that the guy in question was in fact, my high school boyfriend.

I finished getting ready, said goodbye to the boys and told them I would be back later. Then I drove to Rob's house, which was a couple of blocks from where the boys went to elementary school.

Rob and I drove 30 minutes to Rob's mother's house for tea. The last time I was there, I spun my tires in anger on the gravel driveway, intending to never speak to him again as long as I lived. And yet here I was, 30 years later, sitting in his mum's living room, drinking tea and holding his hand. She asked me a lot of questions about this and that, and I answered her truthfully. She was a lovely woman and I had always really liked her.

Our tea date at his mum's came to an end, and Rob and I went to our respective houses. In the days that followed, Rob continued to send pictures of coffee and flowers every morning, along with warm wishes for a wonderful day. We would spend most evenings messaging on our devices as well.

Easter had passed and it was spring. I had been saving my birthday and Christmas money to buy a decent bicycle. My bicycling friend from church had recommended a local bicycle shop, where I purchased a lovely entry level bicycle. I had been riding my tank of a mountain bike, and this bike was so much lighter and faster. It was a dream to ride. I invited Rob for a bike ride and said he could use my mountain bike. He had given up bicycling for martial arts as well. That was all quite nostalgic as in our youth, we had tried but failed to ride our bikes from his mum's house in a neighbouring town to Two Rivers. Here we were, 30 years later, both living in Two Rivers and riding bicycles together.

Greg began to ask a lot of questions about Rob; where he worked, what kind of car he drove, where he lived, and things of that nature. I wondered why he was asking so many questions about it, but he wasn't hostile, so that all seemed reasonable enough. I figured he was 20 years old and had things going on in his own life, so what did he care what I was doing?

I had accepted an invitation from the bicycling lady at church to ride with a group of people in the city I grew up in, about a 30-minute drive from where I lived in Two Rivers. I loaded up my new bicycle and drove off. I rode with the group, and after the ride sent a text to Rob that I was done with the ride and was on my way to his house for a short visit before I went home. Rob's answer to me was that Greg was at his house. I was shocked and thought I'd rather just go home than see my son at Rob's house. I guess Greg and a friend of his had pieced together the tidbits of information I had provided, and with the help of Facebook, had figured out which house was Rob's. I felt completely blindsided that my son would do that. And I wondered *why* he would do that. I also knew he had a very strong personality, and I was concerned about what may have transpired between him and Rob.

Greg went over to Rob's house, introduced himself as my son, and inquired what Rob's intentions were with me. I guess they had a lovely visit. Greg left shortly after I arrived, for which I was grateful as I felt very uncertain about how Greg ended up at Rob's house. I was embarrassed that Greg "caught me going to my boyfriend's house" when I was supposed to be going home after the bike ride. They inquired about the ride, so we chatted very pleasantly, but briefly, and then Greg was on his way.

Greg was a big man and could be very intimidating. Joe, our martial arts instructor, had taken to calling him Thor. I was concerned about what Greg said to Rob and how Rob would feel about that. At that time, Greg and his girlfriend had been together about four years, so he understood a lot about relationships as well, and I knew he had a soft heart under all his rough and tumble demeanour. What, exactly, went on that evening?

Rob told me about their visit, and he thought Greg was a remarkable young man to look out for his mom like that. One of Greg's friends was an aspiring mechanic, and a few days later, he and Greg went to Rob's house and asked to borrow some tools or something. It seemed that Greg was satisfied that this thing with Rob was ok.

Rob began coming to church regularly, and decided he wanted to be baptized. That July, Rob was baptized in the same church where all my sons were baptized, and where Eric's funeral service had been held.

Rob liked my new bicycle, so he and I went to the bicycle shop in the next city and he purchased a new one as well. We spent many happy hours riding our new bicycles on the local trail network, which was amazing. I was so grateful to be able to ride my bicycle again, and even more grateful to be able to share that with Rob, just how we used to when we were young.

When we were teenagers, we talked about getting married when we were old enough. Rob had even given me a ruby and diamond promise ring, which I had kept all those years. We spent a lot of time together that summer of 2017, and decided to get married. It was a whirlwind romance, but we had the benefit of four years of history together, even though that was 30 years prior.

We discussed our thoughts with Pastor Jeff, and he suggested we speak with Pastor Doug, who was also from the church. Pastor Doug specialized in couples counselling and set us up with a marriage course we were to complete, which also had lots of questions for both of us to answer. After that, we had another meeting with Pastor Doug, who reviewed our answers and discussed them with us. Pastor Doug said of all the pre-marital counselling he had done, that he had not had a couple come back as compatible as we had.

In the Bible, God tells us that He will repay us for the years the locust had eaten. There had been a lot of water under the bridge in my life, and in Rob's. The locusts had definitely eaten many of those years. I wonder what a farmer would feel like, seeing a swarm of locusts approaching and be powerless to do anything about it, and then to go and examine the crops after the locusts had moved on and see what had survived, if anything. How devastating would that be? There were times over the years where I felt how that farmer would have felt. Powerless. Devastated. The promise of being repaid for those losses was a promise I was willing to embrace. Instead of powerlessness and devastation, I was embracing hope for prosperity and a future.

JOY IN SPITE OF ADVERSITY

**"Though my father and mother forsake me, the
Lord will receive me" (Psalm 27:10 NIV).**

Kyle applied and was accepted to the science program at the
university, which was about 45 minutes from our house. It
was the same university where he had a tour of the laser lab
when he was in grade nine.

Kyle's birthday was in November, so that meant he started
school when he was quite young. That also meant that he had
graduated from high school and was on his way to university at
the age of 17. The university matched him with a student with
similar interests and background. This young man, Kiran,
was from Capital City, and was in the engineering program.
Kyle and Kiran both loved science and learning, and they
were both from a rural area with lots of property. They both
enjoyed being outdoors and exploring nature. They shared a
two-bedroom dorm, with their own kitchen and bathroom.
Kyle had been doing most of the cooking at home in recent
years, so he knew how to cook, get groceries and all of that,
which he would continue to do at university.

The day we drove him and his stuff to the university
was memorable. He had his car and his stuff, and I had a

few things in my car as well. His brothers came along to see him off too. I knew I was going to be a basket case. I had been reduced to tears on the first day of school every year since Greg's first day of junior kindergarten. We brought Kyle's few things into his furnished room and met his new roommate. With nothing else to be said, his brothers and I left for home before Kyle could see me burst into tears at the thought of leaving him alone in a university that had twice the population of our entire town. He looked somewhat alarmed when we had to leave, but he was a pretty tough customer, so we just said our goodbyes and carried on.

That week, there were lots of activities for the new students to help them meet people and learn their way around the campus. Kyle needed a few things, so the following weekend I drove to the university with those things. When I arrived at his dorm, I was greeted by my precious Kyle wearing full team colours face paint. I believe the idea was to have some black under their eyes like the football players, but for Kyle, if it was worth doing, it was worth overdoing, a concept he learned from his favourite TV show, called Mythbusters. He revealed that he had been riding the city bus around town like that. Kyle had always been his own man and did what he wanted, no matter how outrageous, and didn't care what anyone thought or said. I loved that about him.

That Thanksgiving, my parents and my sister learned Rob and I were getting married. Then things got weird. Christmas was coming up, and my sister called one day to talk about the family getting together for Christmas dinner. She was behaving very oddly. I couldn't put my finger on it, but something was going on. I made some comments about it being hard for me to be with mother, which she knew since I had been very open with her all my life about my relationship with our mother. Then she pulled the pin. She launched into the nastiest tirade I have ever experienced about how horrible I am and things of that nature. The perplexing part was that only a few weeks before at our family Thanksgiving dinner, she spent time telling Rob how much she admired me and looked up to me, and how happy she was for us.

Since I hadn't spoken to her since then, I wondered what happened that her perspective on me had gone in the opposite direction, complete with anger, blame and accusations. A few days later, my father called and wanted to meet with me. He was desperate for us to chat before I was to see him and my mother for my birthday, which was just before Christmas. I agreed to meet with him at a coffee shop. He didn't want Rob to be there—he wanted to speak with just me, which struck me as a bit odd. He knew Rob from when we were young, and we were getting married, so I didn't understand the issue with Rob coming along. I soon learned.

Based on the seemingly endless questions my father asked me about things that had no basis in truth or reality, I began to wonder if my mother and my sister had a conversation about me, my father witnessed it, and he wanted to know what was true. Literally every question he asked me was garbage, and I told him the truth about every situation in question, which was not even close to what he had either been told or overheard about me. I began to get quite agitated. It seemed that my narcissistic mother was angry that I was happy, and that she and my sister had me for lunch, completely devouring me. Thus the unprovoked tirade from my sister. And having that conversation with my father in a public coffee shop meant I was not at home, and there were no witnesses, just how mother liked it.

As my already-planned birthday dinner was only a few days away, Rob and I made our way to the restaurant to meet my parents. Things started off OK. Mother started off a bit cold, but she was speaking to me, so that was something. As our dinner progressed, mother became increasingly angry and mean to me. My father seemed disinterested in speaking to us, looked around the restaurant and did not engage with us very much at all. However, Rob was with me, and I finally had a witness! He was shocked at my mother's behaviour, and I told him that was what I had been dealing with my whole life. Sometimes she was fine, and sometimes she wasn't. She was fine if I was struggling, but whenever I was doing well or was happy, she was flat out mean. Somehow, she always managed to be mean to me when there was no one else there to see it, so I was always left wondering if I had imagined the event, or had understood it wrong. After all, whose mother is angry and mean to their child when the child is happy or successful? I was almost 50! Yet that behaviour was still going on. Bewildered by how my birthday dinner had gone so badly, Rob and I thanked them for the meal and left.

It ended up that none of us were invited to the family Christmas that year, which was fine by me. Not only were we not invited to family Christmas that year, but my family of origin completely disappeared from our lives. They did not send Greg a birthday card in February, or one to Evan for his birthday in May. My sister did not invite us to a Mother's Day event for our mother in May.

We put all of that unpleasant family business behind us and looked forward to our upcoming wedding. I had been married before, and had done the fancy wedding with lots of guests. That was nice then, but in the end a wedding is more about the relationship than the party, as far as I was concerned, so I didn't really want to do that again. The smaller and simpler the better, I thought. Rob agreed and we were married in the same church where so many of my significant life events had taken place. It was a small, simple service on a Sunday afternoon. My family was not invited. We had 20 people there, and all went out for dinner at a local restaurant afterward.

We did everything backwards, according to wedding tradition. We did pictures before the service. I wore red, my very favourite dress that I already owned. We walked down the aisle together as I felt that I was not someone's property to be given away. It was a beautiful service, a lovely dinner, and we had spectacular photographs thanks to Rob's friend, who was a professional photographer.

Rob was gracious enough to move into my house so my sons wouldn't be uprooted. Being married to Rob was truly wonderful and all the difficult things that had happened to me over the years seemed like a distant memory, almost like a movie I had seen long ago, rather than my actual life. He was wonderful with all my sons and had something in common with each of them.

I had in mind an idea of what kind of man I would love to be in a relationship with, and the kind of relationship I would like to have. When I thought of all the things I would love, it occurred to me that a man like that simply did not exist, so I was prepared to be alone for the rest of my life.

However, God, in his uniquely brilliant way with his uniquely brilliant sense of humour, introduced me to the man that was *all* the things I wanted in a man and in a relationship, and more. Only God could have that man be my high school sweetheart, and only God could have made things happen the way they did. Even though I tried to object, and came up with reasons to not get involved, God answered all of those objections, and even had other things in mind that I didn't know I would need.

The Bible tells us that God will receive us even if our father and mother forsake us. That scripture was particularly meaningful to me as my family of origin, my father and mother, abruptly severed ties with me for reasons I didn't know or understand. It was unthinkable to me that parents could be jealous of their child's success and happiness. Even more unthinkable that they would sever ties as a result of that jealousy. Apparently it was a thing, because someone wrote about it and it was included in the Bible. I was very grateful for God's love for me, his protection, his provision, and his acceptance of me, even though my parents had forsaken me.

FREEDOM

"It is for freedom that Christ has set us free. Stand firm then, and do not let yourselves be burdened again by a yoke of slavery" (Gal 5:1 NIV).

Being married to Rob was wonderful. He had been commuting about 45 minutes to his job out of town, but was able to find a job locally, only ten minutes from home, so he was able to come home for lunch every day.

Rob and Greg had developed a great relationship as well. They both loved cars, airplanes, and World War II history. Greg had been working for a well and septic contractor as a plumbing apprentice, and was saving for a house. The year after Rob and I were married, Greg bought a house at the age of 22 and moved out. Only Evan was still at home, as Kyle was away at university. Evan and Rob also developed a great relationship. Rob loved Formula 1 racing, and Evan watched all the races with us. Evan wrote a short story for a school project, which was about a young man who wanted to get into racing. One of the characters in Evan's story was clearly based on Rob.

Two full years passed after the incident with my family, and I hadn't heard from any of them since then. I didn't understand why they were angry with me, and I certainly didn't understand what kind of people didn't even send their own grandchildren birthday or Christmas cards for two years. No contact with me or my sons. I decided since they were clearly angry with me to the point of my not being invited to family Christmas two years prior, there was little point in me trying to contact them either.

A few days before Christmas, I was just home from a client's office and the doorbell rang. It was my parents! They wanted to come in, so I invited them in and asked if they would like some tea. I sent Rob a text that my parents were at our house, and he left work immediately. He understood how different things were for me when there was a witness present. The look on my mother's face was the same one you would see on a dog who had just messed on the carpet. My father behaved as though nothing had happened and expected to just carry on where we had left off two years earlier. I couldn't believe that they would just show up at my house with some cake and cookies, act like nothing had happened, and just expect nothing to be said about that.

Rob arrived home, and the small talk continued. Rob commented that it had been a long time since we had seen them, and mother said she would like to speak to me about that. I said that I would be willing to do that with a counsellor present. The last two years had been pure bliss without having to deal with any of my family of origin. My parents agreed to that. However, the next two months were the busiest for me in my business and I did not want to spend energy on the family entanglements when I needed to be at my best for my work. I strongly doubted any good could come from speaking with them, and since they had snubbed me for two years, what was another couple of months? I felt that since they were the ones who did the snubbing, and they were the ones who wanted to continue the relationship, then they could be the ones to set up a meeting with a counsellor, which they did not do.

My next move was to go and see Pastor John, my go-to father-like figure who had helped me before in times of turmoil. Rob was with me, and I told Pastor John what happened. Rob confirmed what I said and added his perspective as well. Pastor John, having done some family counselling as part of his career in ministry, gave us some helpful suggestions and thought-provoking perspectives, as he always did. I was so very grateful for Pastor John.

I had really enjoyed not having to deal with my family and the uncertainty about whether it would be Jekyll or Hyde who would show up at any given meeting. The struggle I had was with one of the ten commandments, which says to "honour your father and mother, that it may go well with you." As far as I understand, that was the first commandment with a promise. If I didn't honour them, how could it go well for me? After much prayer, reading, and wise counsel from the beloved retired Pastor John, I decided that if anyone else on earth were treating me the way my family treated me, anyone would encourage me to end the relationship. Why should I submit myself to that kind of treatment, just because the people involved were my family? I decided that I could honour my parents by having enough self respect to not allow myself to be mistreated.

It turned out that none of that mattered, as it was another full year before I heard from them. And that was just my dad wanting to meet with me to ask questions about things that had no basis in truth or reality, exactly like the last meeting I had with him a couple of years before. This time, I brought

Rob with me, so I had a witness. I was not sure what the point of that meeting was. Again, I expected that my mother was saying all kinds of things about me, and my father was trying to sort out what was real. I told him again that if he wanted the relationship to continue, I would speak with him and mother with a counsellor present, and if it meant that much to him that he could set that up.

My parents lived in a condominium building that was all retired people. There was a gentleman in the building named Alan who was a retired family counsellor. My father said that Alan was willing to meet with us, but he would like to meet with me first so he could have an understanding of my perspective. He asked that I give some thought to what I wanted to say. I spent some time writing a 20 page document on what I wanted to say, trying to be as clear, concise, and coherent as possible. The day came for me to meet with Alan at his unit. Rob came with me. I told Alan that I would like to just read the document I had prepared in an effort to respect his time and use our time together efficiently. He agreed, and I read.

When I had finished reading the document, Alan sat there with his mouth hanging open. I guessed what he had heard from me was not what he had expected. What I had heard from my father had no basis in truth or reality, and I assumed that Alan had been told the same stories. We spoke about forgiveness and I explained about the work I had done on that after speaking with my retired minister friend. So yes, I had sought wise counsel.

I also spoke about the story of Joseph, again seeking God's model for dealing with situations like the one I was facing. Joseph had been sold into slavery by his brothers, who told their father he had been killed by a wild animal. Joseph was a slave in a neighbouring country, and over time, became the second most powerful man in the country, second only to the king. He was a remarkable man and when the time came for him to be reunited with his brothers, they didn't recognize him. Joseph tested his brothers to see if they were still the same angry bunch of murderous slave traders, or if the school of hard knocks had smoothed off some of their rough edges. That was the golden nugget for me. *Joseph tested his brothers.* If they passed the test, they could be reconciled.

The test I had envisioned for my situation was that if my parents and sister could understand how their behaviour had affected me, and desire to work together for a better relationship in the future, then I would be willing to make another effort. If they were unwilling to change anything, that was their choice. If that was their choice, my choice would then be to not see them again.

Alan summarized by saying, "Unless something changes, there will be no contact."

I agreed. The way I saw it, my parents wanted to continue the relationship, and I was testing to see if that was emotionally safe for me, and willing to try again if they passed the test. If not, I was not about to be "enslaved again under a yoke of slavery I had once put off."

I never heard from Alan, my mother, or my father again. I don't know what happened between Alan and my father after I left that day. I told Alan he could keep the 20 page document I had written on how I felt and why I felt that way. I told him he could show it or even give it to my parents as I had nothing to hide. My take on never hearing from anyone again was that my parents were unwilling to change how they related to me. That was their choice. As agreed with Alan, if my parents didn't want to change how they related to me, then I was done with the relationship. I saw the end of the relationship with my family as their choice. I offered them the choice to do things differently in our relationship, and they did not take it. Not only that, but a meeting with Alan and my parents never even happened. The test was to see if they would make an effort to understand my point of view. They did not want to make that effort, which meant they failed my test.

Forgiveness and reconciliation are a couple of themes in the Bible. If I chose not to see my family again, did that mean I was living in unforgiveness? The thing that was most important to me was to do what was right, as far as God was concerned. And since God wasn't in the habit of sending an email with what I should do, I just muddled along the best I could. I found some wonderful resources on forgiveness. The best thing I could do was pray for my family, and be thankful for the good things I remember. My dad teaching me to ride a bicycle, and to drive, and for helping me with my math homework when I was in high school. Taking me to and from work as a teenager. For all the help they gave me in the early days and years after Eric died.

They truly were not all bad, but the PTSD type of experience I had in the days leading up to, and after, any time I spent with them felt very counterproductive. How could I fly with broken wings? I wanted my wings to be healed, and I wanted to soar. How could I do that if the wings kept breaking over and over? So I prayed for my family, that God would bless them with good health, happiness, peace, and prosperity, and that He would heal whatever was hurting and broken in their lives. I love the book, and movie, *The Shack*. Mack, the main character, was left with debilitating emotional pain, and struggled deeply with forgiving the offender. God told him that forgiveness didn't mean they had to be friends, it just meant Mack had to let go of the offender's throat. I could do that!

Then came the issue of reconciliation. What was God's model for that? Well, in the New Testament, Jesus told his disciples that if they were in a town that did not receive the message they were there to give, to leave the town and shake the dust from their feet. In other words, to "wash their hands" of the situation. I guessed time would tell on that front.

Instead, I signed up for a program by Mary Morrisey. She had an introductory "Dreambuilder" course, which took place over a weekend. The point of the course was to learn about "what I would love." I noticed I had a lot of time once I stopped going to family events and wasn't spending a week on either side of the event gearing up or winding down. It was a place of joy and freedom and I felt like I could use some help on how to move forward. Mary Morrisey's program offered exactly that. I supposed I could also use some healing from the family business, and decided that I had gone as far as I could go as far as growth and thriving were concerned. It was time to reinvent myself again and up my game, and I would need some help with that.

After doing the introductory Dreambuilder weekend course, I signed up for the full program. Before Mary Morrissey founded The Brave Thinking Institute, she obtained a degree in psychology, and was an ordained minister who pastored a church. When she completed her time as minister of the church she founded and began the Brave Thinking Institute, she became a global teacher with the help of the internet. The program was a personal development course, and offered new and empowering ways to think about things. To take control of one's thoughts and decide how to think and be, and move forward intentionally rather than being held captive by poor thinking and being stuck repeating poor choices rooted in deeply entrenched, unhelpful thought patterns. There were daily resources, a box of books, a weekly online teaching session via Zoom, as well as opportunities to ask specific questions of Mary and her team. When I started the program, I didn't even know what I wanted to do with my life. Survival had been the name of the game up until then, and I was in my early 50's. What did I want to accomplish? Who did I want to become? I honestly didn't know when I started Mary's program, and committed to figuring out the answers to those questions and more. I did Mary Morrisey's program for two years, and it changed my life completely.

Rob was able to listen to the Zoom classes with me, and he also attended a free event one time for his own personal growth. Mary's program helped me to verbalize who I wanted to be, and what I wanted to do and have. Everything I verbalized in those two years came true, or something better than I had thought of happened. It reminded me of *Isaiah 43:18, "Forget the former things, do not dwell on the past. See, I am doing a new thing. Now it springs up, do you not perceive it? I am making a way in the desert and streams in the wasteland."*

God can make a way when there is no way. I had already seen that multiple times in my life and wanted to learn how to be, do, and have more. I am so grateful to Mary Morrisey and her team, their program, their teaching, the books they sent, and the daily resources we still enjoy, even though I am no longer signed up for her program. I met some lovely ladies through Mary's program and we have been doing a weekly "Mastermind" call for the past two years. We still meet via Zoom since we live far apart. I treasure these ladies and all we have shared and learned, all the healing and growth we have all experienced.

At the time of writing, Rob and I have just celebrated our sixth wedding anniversary, and our love is better and stronger than it was when we were first married. In fact, a friend recently told us that we look like we are on our honeymoon. God truly is able to do exceedingly, abundantly above and beyond all we could ever dare to hope, ask, or think (Ephesians 3:20).

We fly a checkered flag in our backyard. It is a victory flag, and I have experienced many victories. My wings are healed, and I am soaring.

The Bible tells us that Jesus died to set us free, and to not allow ourselves to be enslaved again under past oppression. That concept was meaningful to me because I saw the way my family treated me as oppression. How could I grow and become when I was spending a significant amount of time and energy trying not to let their behaviour negatively affect me? The idea of not allowing that to continue, not being "enslaved again under past oppression" helped me to feel good about my choice to let my family choose how/if we would move forward in a relationship. Their refusal to honour my feelings was their choice, but I didn't need to continue to allow that dynamic in my life.

ACKNOWLEDGEMENT

I love riding my bicycle—it is a symbol of freedom for me. World Bicycle Relief is an organization created by women. They send heavy duty Buffalo Bicycles to women in developing nations. The women use these bicycles to get to work, to create or expand their business, or to get to school so they can finish their education. Some even become bicycle mechanics and service the bicycles in the area as a business and source of income to support their families. I donate to World Bicycle Relief because I love what they stand for. I love the idea of using a bicycle as a way of giving someone a hand up when their circumstances are challenging. To learn more about what World Bicycle Relief does, you can access their website here: https://worldbicyclerelief.org.

I am forever grateful to the people in my life who provided me with resources and opportunities so I didn't have to stay stuck in a mess. My deepest desire is that you will realize new levels of hope, and gratitude for the people in your life who have provided you with resources and opportunities. A portion of the sale of this book will go to World Bicycle Relief, so women in developing nations are provided with resources and opportunities in the form of a humble, freedom-giving bicycle.

I love reading in Jeremiah 29:11, that God wants to prosper us, and to give us hope and a future. I believe these words are for anyone who will receive them. When we believe it is *possible* for us to prosper, and when we focus our attention on prospering, our prosperity becomes more likely.

What I would like for myself, I would like for everyone; to prosper, have hope and a future.

Self-Publishing School

NOW IT'S YOUR TURN

Discover the EXACT 3-step blueprint you need to become a bestselling author in as little as 3 months.

Self-Publishing School helped me, and now I want them to help you with this FREE resource to begin outlining your book!

Even if you're busy, bad at writing, or don't know where to start, you CAN write a bestseller and build your best life.

With tools and experience across a variety of niches and professions, Self-Publishing School is the only resource you need to take your book to the finish line!

DON'T WAIT

Say "YES" to becoming a bestseller:

https://self-publishingschool.com/friend/

Follow the steps on the page to get a FREE resource to get started on your book and unlock a discount to get started with Self-Publishing School

Can You Help?

Thank You For Reading My Book!

I really appreciate all of your feedback, and
I love hearing what you have to say.

I need your input to make the next version of
this book and my future books better.

Please leave me an honest review on Amazon letting
me know what you thought of the book.

Thanks so much!

H.J. Weiler

ABOUT THE AUTHOR

H.J. Weiler is a fiercely focused multitasker, a (formerly) widowed single parent of three sons, and a woman who knows how to juggle life with grit and grace. A blackbelt, avid cyclist, and business owner, she thrives on challenge—whether it's building a company or chasing sunrises on two wheels. She's the proud steward of her family's lakefront cottage, built by her grandfather in the 1960s, and currently lives in rural Ontario, Canada. There, she shares life (and a lot of laughter) with the love of her life, two cats, and Zorro the ever-opinionated Java sparrow.

www.ingramcontent.com/pod-product-compliance
Lightning Source LLC
Chambersburg PA
CBHW060246050426
42448CB00009B/1582